HOLLYWOODLAND

Also by
David Wallace

Lost Hollywood

DAVID WALLACE

LA
WEEKLY
BOOKS

St. Martin's Press /
An LA Weekly Book
New York

HOLLYWOODLAND

For my son Christopher.

Cover: In 1924, just a few investors and workers gathered on Mt. Lee, high above the film capital, to dedicate a huge sign advertising a new subdivision named Hollywoodland.

All photographs courtesy of Bison Archives except: cover, the Bruce Torrence Hollywood Photograph Collection; title page and page 218 courtesy of the Del Coronado Hotel; page 206 courtesy of the Los Angeles Public Library; and page 198 courtesy of the Del Mar Thoroughbred Club.

Book design by James Sinclair

Library of Congress Cataloging-in-Publication Data

Wallace, David.
        Hollywoodland / David Wallace.—1st ed.
            p. cm.
        Includes index (p. 229)
        ISBN 0-312-29125-6
        1. Motion picture industy—California—Los Angeles—History. 2. Motion picture actors and actresses—United States—Biography. I. Title.
    PN1993.5.U65 W288 2002
    384'.8'097949—dc21

                                                                        2002069829

First Edition: October 2002

10 9 8 7 6 5 4 3 2 1

Contents

Acknowledgments

Writing this book was helped immeasurably by the input of Ann Miller, Esther and Richard Shapiro, Paul Jasmin, Loretta Barrett, Nicholas Mullendore, Elizabeth Beier, Michael Connor, Gregg Sullivan, Marc Wanamaker, and the still lively ghosts of Hollywood.

Foreword

Few subjects have entranced writers as much as the so-called "golden age" of Hollywood, but David Wallace's brilliant new book *Hollywoodland* is clearly the history book of history books about the film capital. No dry history here, though—it's one of the liveliest books you'll ever read, brimming with wonderful, true stories about the dreams and heartbreaks in this town called Hollywood in its greatest years. And no one has given the real lowdown on many of Hollywood's most notorious mysteries and scandals as well as David has.

Here you will discover some of the tragic results of the mob's effort to move in on the film capital a half century ago. Here you will discover why gays and lesbians were forced back into the closet in Hollywood's golden age. I was fascinated with his tales of high society's shenanigans, the inside stories of superstar actresses from Mae West to Jayne Mansfield, and the lonely saga of the Hollywood screenwriter with its decidedly different angle on the last years of F. Scott Fitzgerald. Oh, and if you like clothes like I do, don't miss his captivating chapter about one of my all-time favorite designers of fashions worn in the movies. His name was Adrian and he not only created the "look" that made Joan Crawford famous, he also created one of the movies' most celebrated icons: the ruby red slippers worn by Judy Garland in *The Wizard of Oz*.

But David also did something else. In *Hollywoodland* and his earlier book, *Lost Hollywood*, he somehow has been able to re-create the one element that once defined Hollywood to the world—its glamour.

Today, much of Hollywood and the film industry have been taken over by accountants. But when I first arrived in Hollywood and, lying about my age, made *New Faces of 1937,* the men were the handsomest in the world, the women the most beautiful, the blue Southern California skies were still unsullied by smog, and a legendary director named Frank Capra could cast a young actress (me) in a major role in his Academy Award–winning 1938 film *You Can't Take It with You.* And, ah yes, the parties; they, too, were unbelievable. Dolly Green, one of the daughters of Burton Green who founded Beverly Hills, would often seat me at her huge dining table—itself set with solid gold—alongside such celebrities as Clark Gable, the Maharaja of Jaipur, or Lady Astor.

Like Jane Withers, Shirley Temple, and Mickey Rooney, my costar in *Sugar Babies* from 1979 to 1989, it was my sometimes happy, sometimes frustrating fate to grow up on screen. But, from my first film to my most recent, David Lynch's 2001 movie *Mulholland Drive*, I've survived—better in many ways, I think, than Hollywood itself. Maybe it was my patented "machine-gun" style of tap dancing that kept me in shape, maybe it's because I'm a survivor, who knows? But one thing I do know—to rediscover the

Hollywood of my youth, the glamorous Hollywood that once dazzled the whole world, you must read David Wallace's *Hollywoodland*.

I couldn't put it down.

ANN MILLER

Introduction

When the legends start becoming reality, print the legend.
—Martin Scorsese

Behind every movie you see is a century of tradition. It's a tradition that is as alive and as changing today as it was in the golden age of Hollywood—that era from the 1920s to the arrival of television in the 1950s when some of the greatest (as well as some of the worst) movies were made. It is a body of legend that is seasoned with heartbreak and joy, deceit and honesty, and commonplace work as well as films so inspired they can be numbered among humankind's most memorable artistic achievements.

But Hollywood is more than just a place; it is also a unique environment where many lives have been—and still are—lived far more glamorously and opulently than those of ordinary mortals. So it's not surprising that Hollywood has spawned more anecdotes per capita than probably any other place on earth. For people like myself who love such stories for their sheer fun as well as their ability to bring an entire lost era to life again, dealing with them can be a challenge. Since Hollywood has a habit of exaggerating everything, as well as changing historical facts familiar to millions to fit preconceived storylines (as with 2001's *Pearl Harbor*), you've not only got to find the stories that reanimate a once famous star, event, or a way of life, but also separate fact from fiction created when someone, who knows how many years ago, tried to make a good story better. Since so many of the people actually involved in the great tales of Tinsletown are now in that great movie palace in the sky, my way to reach for the truth behind the anecdotes was to anchor them in known reality; to professions (like screenwriting) and to places and buildings that were significant culturally or physically to Hollywood's tradition (like the huge ranchos that defined the physical growth of Los Angeles, and the dream houses the stars built for themselves).

Hollywood's legends and its reality—like most of history's legends and reality—have also always been defined by its personalities, and they're here: from Harry Cohn, the authoritarian chief of Columbia Pictures once considered the most hated man in Hollywood, to Frank Capra, the seemingly genial director of some of the most beloved films ever made in the film capital. Here, too, are some of the greatest glamour gals of the era; the fashion designers without whom many may not have become famous (Joan Crawford being a perfect example); and, with its triumphs and tragedies, the immensely powerful gay presence in Tinseltown which everyone knew about during Hollywood's golden years but few ever mentioned.

Here, also, are some of the really sad stories of Hollywood, many a product of that endless bane of the film industry from its very beginnings: drugs. And here, too, is a look at Hollywood in its more innocent years, when many of its streets were paved in the springtime by falling orange blossoms.

Of course, the stars had to play, and we'll take a look at some of the places they liked (and that many still like); their favorite golden age avocation of raising, riding and racing horses, and the agents who got them their jobs and hopefully, made and kept them famous.

Nevertheless, the loss of so much that defined golden age Hollywood—the never equaled black-and-white photography many cinematographers mastered in the early years comes to mind—can be discouraging. It is a loss is reflected in a constant litany I hear from both those who can still remember as well as those who can only wonder, for example, what it was that made a Mae West or a Rudolph Valentino so famous.

So it was especially gratifying to discover that, although most of the people who created Hollywood's imperishable legends are gone, many of them are not *lost*, thanks to, of all unexpected rescuers, a thirty-two-year-old Missourian named Tyler Cassity. When Cassity first saw the Hollywood Memorial Cemetery in 1998, the famous sixty-two-acre necropolis that was supposed to be the eternal resting place of a virtual *Almanach de Gotha* of everyone who was anyone during movie's golden era, including Rudolph Valentino, Cecil B. DeMille, Tyrone Power, and Jayne Mansfield (see chapter thirteen)—even the racketeer Benjamin "Bugsy" Siegel—it was a total wreck. Because of fiscal mismanagement, the cemetery was in a total state of overgrown disrepair and was often chained shut. The cemetery's much photographed central lake surrounding a neo-Greek mausoleum on a tiny island was stagnant and scum covered, and even the huge mausoleum where Valentino and a thousand others lie was flooded.

After buying the place for $375,000 and renaming it Hollywood Forever Cemetery, Cassity spent some $3 million upgrading it as both a unique option serving contemporary needs and as a serene park whose residents, famous and otherwise, can continue to rest in peace (it's no accident that Cassity and some of his staff are technical and story-line advisors to the hit HBO series *Six Feet Under*). Then again, his rescue of so much of Hollywood's heritage from what apparently would've been the cemetery's formal abandonment and reassignment to the tender ministrations of the California Parks and Recreation Department (Cemeteryland?) was squarely in the Hollywood tradition of last-minute rescues. But, of course, this time it was for real.

Rescuing some of Hollywood's heritage, in their own modest ways, is what *Hollywoodland* and its predecessor, *Lost Hollywood*, are all about.

HOLLYWOODLAND

In the 1920s, E. L. Doheny, who first hit oil in Los Angeles, was one of America's richest tycoons and a leader of Los Angeles society. But when it was discovered that he had tried to quietly acquire government oil reserves worth millions by bribing President Harding's Secretary of the Interior, the resulting scandal—known as Teapot Dome for the site of one of the reserves—became Washington's biggest before Watergate.

High Society in Tinseltown

If there is a common denominator that seems to define the business of filmmaking in the golden era, "arrogance" is certainly a candidate. Arrogance, of course, comes from insecurity, and how could the early film moguls—many of whom came from the lower reaches of the garment business—not be insecure? Louis B. Mayer actually made his living for a time as a rag merchant after moving to Boston with his new wife in 1904, Samuel Goldwyn sold gloves, Paramount's Adolph Zukor sold furs, and Harry Warner sold shoes. For men of this background who stormed the movie business, arrogance meant survival.

Arrogance was also a defining characteristic of many who thought of themselves as Los Angeles's "high society," the moneyed parvenus who lived in such places as Pasadena and Hancock Park and, from the beginning, looked down their noses at the rough-and-ready film industry. That they boasted origins little better than the filmmakers they disdained was not an issue; their Yellow Pages was the membership lists of such exclusive (and exclusionary) organizations as the Jonathan Club, the California Club, and the Los Angeles Country Club. In effect, they ruled the city and decided its future by any means necessary—both legal and, sometimes, illegal. And their lifestyles, although less well publicized, often far surpassed even those of superstars like Chaplin, Pickford, and Fairbanks in opulence and comfort.

The families at the summit of Los Angeles society included the Chandlers and their once rabble-rousing *Los Angeles Times*; the Rindge/Adamson clan of Malibu, whose matriarch actually barred all public access for years to what is now one of the most famous beachfront communities in the world; and the Dohenys, whose patriarch, once reputedly the richest man in America, also involved America in its most notorious political scandal before Watergate.

The legacy of all three clans is far different than might have been predicted three-quarters of a century ago. The *Los Angeles Times*—if not as good a paper as it became under the 1960 to 1980 stewardship of Otis Chandler, the last member of the family to be its publisher—is tremendously superior to the reactionary and parochial paper it was under his father and grandfather. Today Malibu is a byword for glamour from Arkansas to Zanzibar; its exclusivity and beauty survived because of the Rindge family's determination—in early days enforced by armed riders told to shoot trespassers—to keep the public out. And the library at the University of Southern California, and what must be the most beautiful church in Los Angeles, would never have been built had it not been for the philanthropy of the notorious oilman Edward Doheny, who, in a prequel to the O.J. Simpson trial, avoided going to jail for his crimes by buying a defense team that cost the equivalent of 15 or 20 million of today's dollars.

In 1892, Frederick Hastings Rindge, a philosopher, poet, and writer from Cambridge, Massachusetts, and his wife, May, bought the 13,330-acre Spanish land-grant Malibu Rancho for ten dollars an acre from a financier whose father had purchased it thirty-five years earlier for ten cents an acre (now it would probably cost an average of a hundred thousand an acre). Later expanded to seventeen thousand acres that ran for miles along a south-facing coastline, Rindge's property allowed him to realize a dream he had held all his life: to have "a home near the ocean, under the lee of the mountains, with a trout brook, wild trees, a lake, good soil, and an excellent climate, one not too hot in the summer."

Rindge built a large multigabled and turreted home up Malibu Creek from today's Surfrider Beach, raised cattle and grain, and, in 1898, wrote a book evangelizing his experience, *Happy Days in Southern California*. They were not to remain happy for long. In 1903 his house was destroyed by one of Malibu's still notorious brushfires, and two years later Rindge died at forty-eight, leaving behind three children and a wife who took over the management of his business affairs. They included a life insurance company that he founded, interests in the Union Oil Company and Southern California Edison, and the responsibility of an annual reimbursement of the adjoining city of Santa Monica for the loss of licensing fees after Rindge—a temperance convert—convinced the municipality to abolish saloons.

After Frederick's death, May Rindge built a dam to store water from Malibu Creek and established the famed if short-lived Malibu Potteries. In 1928 she started building the fifty-room Rindge Castle on the twenty-six-acre site of the old ranch house. In 1932, the depression ended construction just short of completion after more than half a million dollars had been spent on hand-carved mahogany stair rails and mantels, marble floors, and gorgeously colored tiles from Malibu factories. But it was her arrogance that earned May Rindge the title Queen of Malibu.

Today Amtrak boasts of the beauty of its coastal route north from Los Angeles. But until one reaches Oxnard, forty-five miles from the city, the coast is nowhere in sight. Why? May Rindge. In 1904, the Southern Pacific applied to the Interstate Commerce Commission to build tracks linking their Los Angeles line, which ended at Santa Monica to their northern tracks, which ended in Santa Barbara. The best route—a direct line—would take the tracks straight through the Rindge's Malibu ranch.

May and Frederick Rindge decided to fight the incursion and discovered that a little known Interstate Commerce Commission law forbid the duplication of an existing railroad line. So they decided to stop the Southern Pacific by building their own railroad. After Frederick's death, May went ahead with the project: a fifteen-mile, standard-gauge railroad named the Hueneme (for Point Hueneme, today a missile test site), Malibu, and Port Los Angeles Railway. Completed in 1908 for $1 million, the Rindge railroad remained in use until the 1920s, hauling grains and hides on flatcars pulled by a small gasoline engine from the ranch to their private shipping wharf (now the Malibu Pier). It never made money, but it did stop the Southern Pacific. As a result, and, unlike many other Southern California coastline cities—among them Santa Barbara—no railroad tracks disfigure the beauty of Malibu's coastline.

The Hueneme, Malibu, and Port Los Angeles Railway was just one shot in May Rindge's generation-long fight to keep the public off her land. She employed litigation, locked gates, injunctions, and even armed riders to keep trespassers off her ranch. The issue—as both Los Angeles County and May Rindge saw it—was simple: the public's right to passage through private lands versus the owner's right to deny it.

In fact, Frederick Rindge erected locked gates on the ranch's wagon road as early as 1894, giving only nearby settlers keys for access. After her husband's death, May Rindge denied all outside access to protect her "privacy and safety," precipitating four California Supreme Court and two U.S. Supreme Court cases demanding that she open the road to the public. Despite public opinion inflamed by newspaper accounts depicting her as "unneighborly" and "selfish," May won the early contests. It was only in 1919 that the County of Los Angeles finally succeeded in getting an order of condemnation for the right-of-way and began construction of a road. Even then May kept fighting, locking gates near the present intersection of Pacific Coast Highway and Las Flores Canyon and, after the road was completed, petitioning the U.S. District Court for a restraining order. All she achieved was to delay an opening that finally took place on November 21, 1921. Then the state decided to build its own road along the coast, only to be met by forty of May's armed guards on horseback and the familiar flurry of legal blockades. Not until 1929—twenty-two turbulent years after May Ringe first went to court to keep people off her land—did the Roosevelt Highway, now the Pacific Coast Highway, open to everyone.

Actually, the Roosevelt Highway benefited May Rindge by easing access for the large labor pool by the Malibu Potteries that she started in 1926. Located along fifteen hundred feet of beachfront a half mile east of the pier (not far from today's celebrity-studded Carbon Beach enclave, which includes billionaire David Geffen's home), the company manufactured thirty thousand square feet per month of the brightly colored, Mediterranean-inspired tile favored at the time by architects and designers in the Los Angeles basin, especially for homes in Hollywood subdivisions such as Whitley Heights and Hollywoodland. And tiles from the pottery were not only restricted to homes: Twenty-three large decorative tile panels were installed in 1928 in the Los Angeles City Hall, and a pair of huge tile murals picturing William Henry Dana's ship, *The Pilgrim*, arriving in San Pedro Bay in 1834, were installed in the city's Dana Junior High School the same year. Malibu Pottery tiles also found their way into one of Los Angeles's most famous landmarks. It is said that Simon Rodia, builder of the fantastical Watts Towers, once worked at the pottery and would often fill his pockets with broken tile fragments that would end up decorating his now landmarked creations.

The pottery was destroyed by fire in 1931, and despite May's promises to rebuild it, the Great Depression stopped her as effectively as it stopped completion of her "castle." After May died, practically insolvent, on February 8, 1941, her "castle" and thousands of tiles stored there were sold for fifty thousand dollars to the Franciscan monks, who expanded and reopened it as a retreat house. In 1970, virtually everything was destroyed in yet another brushfire.

Among the most remarkable artifacts lost when May's "castle" burned was a huge Persian carpet created entirely out of Malibu Potteries tile, but another example exists in the house built nearby in 1929 by May and Frederick's daughter, Rhoda, and her husband, a lawyer named Merritt Huntley Adamson. Now run by the State of California as the Malibu Lagoon Museum, the place is one of the most remarkable homes in America, spectacularly situated on an outpoint of land on the ocean at Surfrider Beach on a slight rise once known as Vaquero (Cowboy) Hill. Used as a weekend beach house while the couple still lived in their Hancock Park mansion, it became their permanent residence in 1936.

Visiting the Malibu Lagoon Museum is like taking a time machine to Hollywood's golden age. Each room of the five-bedroom house is preserved as it was when the Adamsons lived there, and even the bedroom closets are still stocked with Rhoda's dresses from I. Magnin's (she always bought a variety of colors of a design she liked). The kitchen icebox contains old milk bottles bearing the name of the once-famous family-owned dairy, Adohr Farms (Rhoda's name spelled backward). In addition to the famous tile carpet, examples of Malibu Potteries tiles are everywhere, from the table in the front hall to the spectacular peacock (with one tile set upside down because Rhoda felt only God could create something perfect) on the outdoor fountain to the built-in settee on the balcony, cleverly warmed during winter months by heat from the house's fireplace flues. The pool used to be filled with salt water and changed four times a week, but this practice stopped during World War II when the Coast Guard took over the pool house. The gardens are still filled with hundreds of rose-bushes, as they were in Rhoda Adamson's time, and sheltering much of the property is a century-old, spectacularly colored coral tree, said to be the largest in America.

There is, of course, a delicious irony in all this: May Rindge, a woman who fought arrogantly to keep the public off her Malibu land, ended up preserving that land so that it would one day become a world-famous tourist destination.

If the Rindge/Adamson clan can be said to have given us the modern Malibu by blocking "progress" at a crucial time, another family—at least one of its most prominent members—can be said to have given us, for good or evil, much of today's Los Angeles. The name is Harry Chandler, and his instrument of power was the family-run *Los Angeles Times*.

"The *Times* is not a public institution, run in the service of the people. It is a private institution run for the personal business advantage . . . it is even worse than this; it is an instrument for the promotion of Mr. Chandler's unpatriotic enterprises and crooked deals. In other words, the newspaper is being prostituted for the private unworthy ends of its proprietor." Strong words, indeed, from William Randolph Hearst, whose *Los Angeles Examiner*, as well as his many other newspapers, could hardly be accused of objectivity. Actually, until the fourth generation took over the paper's reins in 1960, the *Times* regularly appeared on lists of the ten worst newspapers in the country. Humorist S. J. Perelman had once famously declared that on a train trip to California, he asked a porter for a newspaper "and unfortunately the poor man, hard of hearing, brought me the *Los Angeles Times*." In more recent times, the late broadcaster Chet Huntley observed that by reading the *Los Angeles Times* he knew he could find the truth "by going 180 degrees in the other direction."

For generations, the paper's partisanship knew no bounds. In 1934, after the muckraker Upton Sinclair captured the Democratic nomination for governor and appeared headed for victory in November, the paper's political editor, Kyle Palmer, told a visiting reporter from the *New York Times*, Turner Catledge, "We don't go in for . . . being obliged to print both sides." He promised that his paper—until recently also a bastion of Republican politics—would "kill" Sinclair politically (and it did). Sixteen years later, Palmer, still a political kingmaker, wrote that his paper would promote the Senate candidacy of Richard M. Nixon, allowing that "from time to time, as space allows," it might also cover his rival, Helen Gaha-gan Douglas.

Printing the news was considered less important than promoting the growth of Los Angeles, which included campaigning projects such as the creation of a deepwater port in San Pedro and a reliable supply of water. Many of the improvements the paper supported were generally beneficial to the city and its growth, unless, of course, you were on the wrong end of the deal, like the farmers of the Owens Valley who watched their land dry up as water was siphoned off for Los Angeles. That it just so happened the publisher was usually part of a syndicate profiting by that growth was not much different from similar schemes in an age less concerned about business ethics. Harry Chandler's father-in-law, General Harrison Gray Otis, owned or controlled the ownership of 1.5 million acres in what would become Hollywood as well as in the gigantic San Fernando Valley. To make certain everyone knew about the easy life in Los Angeles, in 1886 the *Times* started printing a special midwinter edition (in 1890 it included the first stories about Pasadena's Tournament of Roses parade) and distributing it free to thousands of readers throughout the snowbound east. Not surprisingly, the midwinter edition was soon carrying more advertising than any paper in the country.

When Harrison Gray Otis, then an Ohio publisher, bought a one-quarter interest in the *Los Angeles Daily Times* (circulation four hundred) in 1882, his timing was perfect. The Southern Pacific Railroad had finally made possible direct shipments of the area's bounty—then mostly oranges and wine—to the east six years earlier, and the population had grown from five thousand to over twelve thousand. That same year, writer Helen Hunt Jackson vacationed in the town, and was soon to begin a parade of the romanticized portrayals of the place as a make-believe Eden with her best-selling 1884 novel, *Ramona*. About that time, a nineteen-year-old Dartmouth student named Harry Chandler, suffering from tuberculosis, dropped out of school, moved to Los Angeles to regain his health, and took a twelve-dollar-a-week job in the *Times'* circulation department. He had to physically bundle and load the then three thousand papers printed daily onto wagons (which cured his tuberculosis in short order), and soon he bought a 1,400-subscriber delivery route, then a freelance distribution system serviced by a crew of newsboys.

In 1894 Chandler married Otis's daughter, Marian, and a pattern of succession that was to endure for nearly a century was cemented; Harry became publisher of the paper in 1917 on Otis's death, their first child, Norman, born in 1899, succeeded him in 1944, with his son Otis following Norman in 1960.

The story of the warfare between industry and the unions at the beginning of the twentieth century has been often told, and, like Henry Ford and his friend (and occasional syndicate partner) Harvey Firestone, Otis loathed the unions and everything they represented. He took every opportunity he could to keep them out of the city, both through the city's Merchants and Manufacturers Association and through the police who enforced a clearly unconstitutional anti-picketing ordinance passed by a *Times*-friendly city council. At 1:07 A.M. on October 1, 1910, a gigantic explosion ripped through the huge *Times* building which the militarily inclined Otis—a retired general—called the "fortress" and which was stocked with dozens of rifles. Twenty-one employees were cremated in the fire that followed. Otis himself was out of town, but Harry Chandler, who often worked late, had left only an hour before. It was rightly suspected that the explosion had been the work of pro-union dynamiters, and it wasn't long before an alcoholic itinerant printer named James B. McNamara and his brother

John were tracked down by William J. Burns (founder of the Burns Detective Agency) and indicted for the crime. Despite a vigorous defense mounted by the celebrated lawyer Clarence Darrow, the pair were found guilty, receiving jail sentences in lieu of execution though a plea bargain. (John was paroled in 1921 and remained an outspoken union supporter for the rest of this life; James died in San Quentin in 1941.)

In the early 1920s, when a series of celebrity scandals rocked Hollywood, the Chandlers, strict Congregationalists, supported the industry's effort to save Hollywood from itself by recruiting through the *Times'* bureau President Warren G. Harding's post-master general, Will Hays, to set up and enforce a code of conduct.

In 1921, the *Los Angeles Times* launched the nation's first regular movie coverage with a section—eventually a sixteen-page Sunday supplement—called *The Preview*. At the same time, the paper hired the first Hollywood gossip columnist, who wrote anonymously under the byline "Stella the Star Gazer." But not long after such scandals as William Desmond Taylor's murder and the death of Virginia Rappe in Roscoe (Fatty) Arbuckle's hotel suite broke, he dropped the gossip column as well as the special section. It was one of Harry Chandler's few mistakes, as it left the newly popular gossip field wide open for Hearst and his new columnist, Louella Parsons. Not for a decade and a half would Chandler and the *Times* reenter the gossip wars by hiring Parsons's great rival, Hedda Hopper.

As opportunistic as the Chandler clan's fortune building was, most of the horse-trading was done behind closed doors. So, too, was the deal cut with the U.S. government in the early 1920s by oilman

Edward Doheny, though—unlike much of Otis's and Harry Chandler's scheming—the door was soon flung open for all the world to see on Doheny's scheme to make millions. Until Watergate came along, the resulting scandal was the greatest to rock Washington in the twentieth century; seventy-five years later, the name for the scandal is still a metaphor for corruption, even if most people don't remember exactly why: Teapot Dome.

In 1892, newly arrived from Wisconsin and almost broke, Edward L. Doheny Sr. was, according to legend, the very first person to strike oil in Los Angeles. Doheny, the story goes, was in the downtown area when he noticed a cart rolling by with a black substance on its wheels. When he asked the driver where he had come from, the man pointed in a northwest direction. Doheny investigated and, in partnership with his previous goldmining partner, Charles Canfield, borrowed four hundred dollars to buy one thousand acres of land near the intersection of Glendale Boulevard and Beverly Boulevard in the Echo Park neighborhood. After digging a five- by seven-foot shaft by hand to a depth of 150 feet, the pair then used a sharpened eucalyptus trunk to drill still deeper. On November 4, 1892, they struck oil at 460 feet, first bailing out seven barrels a day in a bucket. Production quickly increased to forty-five barrels a day, and when the word got around that Los Angeles was sitting on a gigantic petroleum reserve, one of the biggest land booms in the country's history erupted and Doheny was on his way to becoming the richest man in America.

The original derrick-covered field has long since disappeared, but not the memory of Edward Doheny, who, within a few years when the market was glutted, bought up leases at pennies on the dollar and expanded his explorations to nearby Fullerton, California, and Mexico, where he soon brought in the biggest gusher in the country's history. Then, in the early 1920s, when his eighty-one wells were pumping 6 million barrels of oil daily and producing an annual income of $10 million, he fatefully expanded his vision to the Kern River Valley, one hundred miles north of Los Angeles.

It was 1921, and the hapless Warren G. Harding was president of the United States; his secretary of the interior was another former gold prospecting associate of Doheny's named Albert Bacon Fall. During the earlier administration of William Howard Taft, the U.S. Navy had been awarded almost eighty thousand acres of proven oil lands to be tapped for fuel in the event of a national defense emergency. These fields were in Wyoming at a place called Teapot Dome and in a place where Doheny had already smelled oil called Elk Hills in Kern County.

Doheny convinced Fall as well as the secretary of the navy, Edwin Denby, that the navy's oil was being siphoned off by neighboring drillers and that to prevent this from continuing, the Kern County leases should be transferred (without competitive bidding) to Doheny's Pan American Petroleum, who would drill, refine, and transfer the oil to storage tanks he would also build for the navy in Pearl Harbor. To make everything look less suspicious, Fall insisted on also transferring the navy properties in Wyoming to another oil tycoon, Harry Sinclair (for a payment of four hundred thousand dollars in cash and securities plus livestock and a prize horse for Fall's New Mexico ranch). To close the deal, Doheny had his son, Edward Doheny Jr., and his son's longtime chauffer, friend and personal secretary Hugh Plunkett, deliver a suitcase containing a hundred thousand dollars in cash to Fall in Washington. From the estimated reserves of 75 to 250 million barrels he "leased" for that hundred thousand plus the estimated $5 million to $6 million cost for building the Pearl Harbor facilities, Doheny told his associates only bad luck would prevent him from making "$100 million in profit."

But Doheny's gusher was about to explode. In 1923, Fall decided to retire, presumably because he was hearing rumblings of corruption. (Harding offered him an appointment to the Supreme Court, which he declined.) Then, in August of that year, Harding died under somewhat mysterious circumstances while visiting San Francisco (the Surgeon General diagnosed it as food poisoning; friends thought it was a stroke induced by his high blood pressure; enemies suggested that his wife, Florence, poisoned him because of his notorious philandering). The new president was the shy, intellectual, and completely honest Calvin Coolidge, and it was not long before a Senate committee began investigations into the transfers of the navy's oil reserves. Among the first witnesses were the retired Albert Fall and Edward Doheny Sr., both of whom denied any money had passed between them. Three years later, for reasons that are still speculation, Doheny, then sixty-seven, recanted his original testimony and admitted he had given Fall the hundred thousand as a loan.

In 1929, two years after the government invalidated the Elk Hills and Teapot Dome leases, Fall was convicted of accepting a bribe; Doheny, thanks to a defense that cost him $1 million—$15 million in today's money—was acquitted of giving one. Sinclair received a short sentence for jury tampering.

In 1893, the year after he hit oil, Doheny married Carrie Betzhold; their only child, Edward Jr. (always called Ted) was born that year. In 1900, Carrie reportedly "disappeared"; she in fact committed suicide by drinking battery acid. Edward Sr. then remarried; his second wife was also named Carrie, and together they embarked on a campaign of philanthropy rarely matched anywhere. They also built several celebrated homes, one now the site of a local college, the other the largest ever built in Beverly Hills, today the headquarters of the American Film Institute, and a familiar location seen in many films.

Their home, the flamboyantly Victorian Doheny Mansion on Chester Place, in an exclusive residential district near downtown developed by Doheny, was bought in 1901. After Edward's death in 1935, Carrie continued to live there until her death in 1958, when the house was left to the Catholic Church (it is now the Doheny campus of Mount St. Mary's College). In 1925, the couple provided the funding to build the nearby St. Vincent de Paul Church, one of the most spectacular examples of Spanish baroque style architecture to be found in America. That year, they also began construction of what would be the largest home ever constructed in Beverly Hills as a gift to their son. Built on twenty-two acres of a 429-acre tract the elder Doheny bought in 1910, the 46,500-square-foot, fifty-five-room mansion was built in a high Tudor style of gray limestone (hence its name, Greystone). It would take three years to complete at a cost of $3.1 million (over $30 million today).

On February 16, 1929, only six months after Doheny Jr., his wife, and five children moved into Greystone, Doheny's wife, Lucy, found him in a guest bedroom near death from a gunshot wound to the head. Hugh Plunkett, Ted's friend and secretary who had accompanied him to Washington to deliver the Teapot Dome bribe for Fall, was standing nearby, holding a .45 caliber pistol When confronted by Lucy and the family doctor, Plunkett, who was on medication for a nervous disorder, turned the gun on himself and committed suicide.

The media had a field day with the story. Among the rumors that immediately surfaced was the story that Plunkett and Doheny were more than just "good friends," and that a jealous Lucy killed them both. Another claimed Plunkett shot Doheny in a quarrel over his salary. Still another, that Plunkett was blackmailing the Dohenys to keep quiet about the payoff to Fall (the trial was coming to a head when the deaths occurred). Questions were raised about the timing of the killings: Some said there was a four-hour delay between the time of the deaths and the arrival of the police. It was rumored that the deaths occurred in the master suite and the bodies had been moved to the guest room before the police were called to perhaps better suit the family's scenario. Was there an effort made to make Plunkett look crazy, to make a murder/suicide scenario more plausible? And what about the rumored powder stains on Doheny's hand . . . who really shot whom?

No movie was ever made about the Dohenys, but several have been made in Greystone. Among them: 1993's *Indecent Proposal* (it's the house real estate broker Demi Moore shows Robert Redford—he didn't like it); *What Women Want* (with Mel Gibson), *The Bodyguard* (starring Kevin Costner and Whitney Houston), *The Witches of Eastwick* (Jack Nicholson and Cher), *Ghostbusters II* (Dan Ackroyd and Bill Murray), *Death Becomes Her* (Goldie Hawn and Meryl Streep); *Jumpin' Jack Flash* (Whoopie Goldberg), *Air Force One*, *Nixon*, and *Batman and Robin*.

Edward Doheny Jr. had graduated from USC in 1916, and after his return from serving in the navy in World War I, he served as president of the school's alumni association. So it was understandable that when the Dohenys wanted to memorialize their son after his death, they would do so at his school. The result was the Edward L. Doheny Jr. Memorial Library, built in 1932 for $1.1 million. Mrs. Doheny also gave her rare book collection to St. John's Seminary in Camarillo.

The shenanigans of the Doheny, Chandler, and Rindge clans are of course not isolated. There are countless other examples of social and legal swashbuckling on the screen. But the amazing thing is that so many acts motivated by greed or selfishness or fear or revenge eventually contributed to the common good. Such relatively happy endings to bad beginnings are not unique to Hollywood or Southern California; the experience has been paralleled in other countries around the world. The difference is that these families were prominent in Hollywood, the great magnifying glass of culture for the past century.

Thelma Todd was a popular comedienne, starring in more than 120 films in the 1920s and early 1930s, including a number of Hal Roach and Marx Brothers comedies. Her boyfriend was "Lucky" Luciano, and after she refused to let him turn an oceanside restaurant she owned into a casino, she died. Her death has never been solved, but many believe it was a hit ordered by her lover.

The Mob Moves in and "Hot Toddy" Dies

The widespread corruption in the Los Angeles police force and district attorney's office during the golden age of Hollywood has often been mined by writers, perhaps never better than in James Ellroy's novel *L.A. Confidential*. Although Ellroy may have taken it a bit over the top, it's true that for years the people charged with protecting the citizens of Tinseltown as well as those charged with prosecuting lawbreakers often did just the opposite: accepting payoffs to cover up the facts, helping powerful studio chiefs to protect an actor's reputation, or just looking the other way—an early example of "don't ask, don't tell." These were all a symptoms of an illness that over the next generation would allow gangsters from New York, Chicago, and Detroit to invade the film capital and corner millions of dollars from the drug, numbers, and protection rackets.

In his time, the person most responsible for this laissez-faire attitude was a World War I veteran and

American Legion leader named Buron Fitts. First deputy district attorney of L.A. County, then lieutenant governor of California from 1927 until 1929, and district attorney from 1928 until 1940 (the longest serving DA in the city's history), during which time he prosecuted his predecessor, Asa Keyes, on bribery charges. This was despite his being largely known for taking bribes himself, especially during and after covering up the facts in the notorious William Desmond Taylor murder case in 1922.

As writer Budd Schulberg said during a recent centenary F. Scott Fitzgerald seminar at USC: "I always thought of Hollywood like a principality of its own. It was like a sort of a Luxembourg or a Liechtenstein. And the people who ran it really had that attitude. They weren't only running a studio; they were running a whole little world. Their power was absolutely enormous, and it wasn't only the power to make movies or to anoint someone or make someone a movie star or pick an unknown director and make him famous overnight. They could cover up a murder. Burton Fitts, the district attorney, was completely in the pocket of the producers. You could literally have somebody killed, and it wouldn't be in the papers. They ran this place." During World War II, Fitts joined the army air force and commanded operations in Africa and Europe; on March 29, 1973, he committed suicide. The gun he used, an old .38 Smith and Wesson revolver, was identical to that used by Mary Miles Minter's mother, Carol Shelby, to kill Taylor more than fifty years earlier and never seen since.

On December 16, 1935, a thirty-year-old actress named Thelma Todd, nicknamed "Hot Toddy" because of her devil-may-care lifestyle, was found dead at the wheel of her chocolate-brown Lincoln convertible, dressed to the hilt and wearing twenty thousand dollars in jewels. The car was parked in the Pacific Palisades garage of director Roland West. The inquest concluded that Todd died from "carbon monoxide poisoning." Everyone in Hollywood considered it a convenient cover-up for murder. Her death still stands as one of Hollywood's most famous unsolved mysteries.

Todd, born in 1905, was one of the film industry's most popular comediennes during the late 1920s and early 1930s. A wisecracking platinum blond who appeared in over 120 movies, she is best remembered today for her roles in the Marx Brothers' movies *Monkey Business* and *Horse Feathers*, as well as for costarring with ZaSu Pitts in a number of Hal Roach comedies. In 1932 she married millionaire playboy, self-proclaimed agent, and Charles "Lucky" Luciano chum Pasquale (Pat) DiCicco.

In August 1934, Todd opened Thelma Todd's Sidewalk Café in a still-standing building bought by West, who was then her lover (she had quickly given up being faithful to Pat), on the Roosevelt Highway (now the Pacific Coast Highway) in Pacific Palisades. West, famous at the time for 1926's *The Bat* (in which he also costarred with his estranged wife, Jewel Carmen), a Norma Talmadge melodrama called *The Dove* (1927), and *The Bat*'s talkie sequel, *The Bat Whispers* (1931), lived in a sprawling Spanish-style house on Posetano Road on the Palisades, 270 cement steps above the restaurant where Todd also had an apartment. Despite being packed with friends like Clark Gable and Spencer Tracy, the place was constantly in the red, due to Todd's and West's dismal business sense.

Early in Todd's marriage, DiCicco introduced her to Luciano (then also known as "Charlie Lucifer" because of his reputation as a merciless killer) at the Brown Derby. Like his hated enemy, Capone partner Frank Nitti, Luciano decided that the film capital was ripe for plucking; soon he largely controlled the drug traffic in the city and decided to move in on gambling. It wasn't long before Todd and Luciano, despite a stormy relationship, were sexually intimate.

Luciano's plan to corner the gambling activities of Hollywood's high rollers was, to say the least, unorthodox. In late 1935 Luciano began to pressure West to rent him the third floor of the Sidewalk Cafe, hitherto used for storage, for a casino. His thinking was that the many celebrities who packed Todd's restaurant would welcome such a convenience. West turned him down cold, but Luciano was so persistent that West decided to sell the place. Todd had a better idea. She would turn the third floor into a steakhouse and open it in time for New Year's celebrations. Frustrated and drinking heavily because of the pressure (Luciano had even gone so far as to threaten her life during an argument, again at the Brown Derby), Todd at last gave way to her mother's suggestion that she see the police. Apparently unaware of Burton Fitts's corrupt reputation, she made an appointment to meet with the district attorney at 11:30 A.M. on December 17.

The night of Todd's death she had dinner with Luciano, during which he demanded to know why she called the DA. First she denied making the call, then told him she was going to spill the beans about his underground dealings. The couple was spotted late that night driving her Lincoln convertible toward the Palisades. Luciano left Los Angeles on a flight to New York at seven forty-five the next morning, never to return to the City of the Angels. Despite a call from the Ogden Utah police chief who claimed he was in contact with a person who claimed to know the identity of the killer, the Los Angeles police never followed up on the crime; by then the case had long been closed. Pat DiCicco, who was a suspect for a while in Todd's death, married the seventeen-year-old Gloria Vanderbilt in 1939 (when they divorced three years later, her family paid him a reported five hundred thousand dollars to stay out of the way). On his deathbed, West confessed that he had killed Todd, but his confession was dismissed as the ravings of a sick man. Who killed "Hot Toddy"? Most believe it was probably a hit ordered by Luciano through Detroit's infamous Purple Gang.

Less than two years later, a former Murder, Inc. soldier and Luciano friend named Benny "Bugsy" Siegel rang the doorbell of a thirty-five-room white brick mansion in Holmby Hills and told the owner, the celebrated Metropolitan Opera baritone Lawrence Tibbett, that he would give him two hundred thousand dollars for his house provided he vacated the premises within twenty-four hours. Without batting an eyelid, Tibbett took the deal; it was far more than the house was worth and also, considering the fact that Siegel was then one of the most infamous mobsters in the country, it was an offer he couldn't refuse. That, at least, is the story, but the truth is he might have simply rented the place from Tibbett.

Siegel and his longtime friend Meyer Lansky, a man whose business smarts made him one of the two or three most powerful figures in organized crime, controlled a gigantic gambling empire in Florida and smelled big money in Hollywood. They may have envied another group who had already hit Hollywood: Backed by Capone associate Frank ("the Enforcer") Nitti, Chicagoans Willie Bioff and George Browne controlled the powerful International Alliance of Theatrical Stage Employees and Motion Picture Operators union (IATSE) and had made a fine art of forcing payoffs from theater chains (usually twenty-five thousand from Poverty Row producers, and up to a hundred thousand from major studios) to avoid strikes by projectionists. (MGM's Sam Goldwyn, however, refused to bow to the threats with the famous malapropism "Gentlemen, include me out.")

In 1937, Siegel—who had visited the Coast several times previously—moved permanently to Hollywood determined to gain control of gambling and prostitution. He also grabbed control of the extras' union; an extras' strike would be every bit as devastating as a strike by Bioff and Browne's IATSE. And, like Bioff and Browne, Siegel began accepting "loans" from producers. Dubbed a "New York playboy" by Hollywood media, who were reluctant to say anything negative about anyone involved in the industry, Siegel palled around with George Raft, who opened many industry doors for the gangster, and also began dating the Countess de Frasso (then on the rebound from Gary Cooper), who knew everyone who was anyone in the film industry.

Publisher William Randolph Hearst, however, wasn't one to avoid conflict (unless, of course, it directly affected him or his mistress, Marion Davies), and it was not long before his *Los Angeles Examiner* began to hint at Siegel's mob connections. In 1940, the top was off the media after Siegel was booked for the murder of a hood named Harry Greenberg (whose real name was Harry Schachter), a former Murder, Inc. syndicate member who fled New York when New York DA Tom Dewey cracked down on the operation. Greenberg had threatened to talk unless he was paid off and, then realizing his mistake, fled west as far as he could go. The arm of Murder, Inc. was long, though; Siegel was contacted and told to help their hit man—Allie "Tick Tock" Tannenbaum—make the hit that took place outside "Greenie's" still-standing Hollywood apartment at the intersection of Yucca St. and Vista del Mar. His death had the dubious distinction of being Murder, Inc.'s first hit in California. Siegel was cleared after a witness "fell" from a hotel window.

With World War II came the added opportunity of the black market, whose goods—usually rationed—found willing customers throughout the industry. To reciprocate and provide Hollywood with a new showcase, Siegel decided to develop a showcase casino-resort named the Flamingo in a dusty little community conveniently located only hours away in Nevada—Las Vegas (the project began as a partnership with *Hollywood Reporter* owner Billy Wilkerson, whom Siegel soon bought out). Despite opening at Christmas, 1946, with headliners Jimmy Durante, Xavier Cugat, and George Jessel and dozens of celebrity guests such as Clark Gable, Lana Turner, Joan Crawford, and Cesar Romero, the place was a bust, leaking money, as one reporter said, "like blood from a Murder, Inc. victim."

No one really knows what finally convinced Siegel's mob backers (from whom he had borrowed most of the money to build the Flamingo; originally pegged to cost $1.2 million, the costs spiraled up to $6 million) to get rid of him, but it was probably a combination of several things. First, the disappointment over the Flamingo as a moneymaker (eventually, of course, it turned into a hugely profitable operation for the Hilton chain). Also, one of Siegel's original assignments when he moved west was to get California bookmakers to leave a rival wire service (which gave bookmakers early news on horse races) and subscribe to a syndicate-backed service. He did so but then refused to share the profits with the east coast, virtually daring the syndicate to come and get him.

At 10:30 P.M. on the night of June 29, 1947, bullets from a 30-06 crashed through the window of actress Virginia Hill's Beverly Hills house, where Bugsy was staying (while Virginia, Siegel's girlfriend, was in Europe. The Flamingo hotel was named after her long legs). The first bullet hit him square in the eye. Four more tore up his lungs, but by then Bugsy Siegel was very dead. One of the first people in the house after Siegel's assassination was Hearst reporter Florabel Muir; she found his eyelid stuck to the fireplace with drying blood. It was later discovered that Siegel's death sentence had been ordered by his friends Meyer Lansky (who later confided that he had no choice), and Charles "Lucky" Luciano.

That would have been no problem for Luciano. Despite the ties friendship, Luciano was ruthless, and to his thinking the Siegel problem demanded ruthlessness. It was the same kind of ruthlessness he demonstrated when he cold-bloodedly ordered Hot Toddy killed in 1935.

It was in Hollywood that F. Scott Fitzgerald—several biographies to the contrary—would find again the prosperity of his *Great Gatsby* days, as well as the love of a devoted companion. He and his lover, columnist Sheilah Graham, were photographed in 1938 by a friend in the backyard of the house in Encino (rented from character actor Edward Everett Horton) where they lived for a year and a half before moving back to Hollywood.

The Lowest of the Low—
The Hollywood Screenwriter

It's December 1940, and in a fairly plain apartment located on North Laurel Street just around the corner from Sunset Boulevard and Schwab's Drugstore, the social center of the neighborhood, a prematurely frail, forty-four-year-old writer was spending most of his time in bed, able to work only two or three hours a day on a novel at a special desk he had built to fit around his bed. He would soon die and the apartment would become only a memory, replaced by the same large shopping mall that devoured Schwab's where, a month earlier the writer had suffered a "cardiac spasm" while buying a pack of cigarettes. After his death, the obituaries were condescending, relegating him to the dustbin of literature. Friends including Dorothy Parker, Robert Benchley, and John O'Hara, who believed in his true genius, were infuriated. Now, of course, F. Scott Fitzgerald is recognized as one of America's greatest writers, and the novel he was working on when he died, *The Love of the Last Tycoon*, albeit unfinished, remains one of the best about Hollywood in the 1930s, right up there with Nathanael West's *The Day of the Locust*.

Before Fitzgerald's fatal heart attack on December 21, suffered while he was eating a Hershey bar in the nearby home of his lover, columnist Sheilah Graham, the writer had tried three times to make a success in Hollywood—in 1927, in 1931, and, for three and a half years since being offered a contract by MGM in July 1937. Despite the romantic story that he was a failure leading a sad and grubby life in Hollywood and drinking himself to death, the fact is that—occasional drinking binges aside—Fitzgerald was doing pretty well during his final stay in Hollywood. Since signing the contract with MGM, he had earned some ninety-one thousand dollars (nearly a million dollars today), about the same as his average twenty-five-thousand-dollar annual income during *The Great Gatsby* heyday of the 1920s. Not only was he able to pay off a decade's accrual of debts amounting to over forty thousand, as well as pay his wife Zelda's hospital bills at the Highland Sanitarium in Asheville, North Carolina, according to most contemporary reports he was fairly happy, felt his creative juices flowing again, and was sharing his life with an indulgent, loving companion. It was later biographers who painted his final years as relentlessly tragic.

Of course, like thousands of writers before and since, Fitzgerald was frequently angry and frustrated over the way he was treated in the film industry. In all of the time he spent in the film capital his name was attached to only one film, MGM's 1938 production of *Three Comrades*, based on Erich Maria Remarque's best-selling novel and starring Robert Taylor, Robert Young, Franchot Tone, and Margaret Sullavan. And even that script, to Fitzgerald's undying fury, was revised by its producer, the then screenwriter Joseph Mankiewicz, to remove, the author firmly believed, all his subtleties. Fitzgerald called Mankiewicz "Monkeybitch"; he is perhaps best remembered today for producing 1940's *The Philadelphia Story* (directed by George Cukor) and winning the Best Director and Best Screenplay Oscars for 1950's *All About Eve*.

But Fitzgerald knew how Hollywood worked, and that knowledge helped make *The Last Tycoon* so good, full of scenes of laser-sharp honesty describing moviemaking in the 1930s. Inseparable was his understanding of the writer's plight in an industry that, when it began, needed scenario writers (not script writers in that silent era) to crank out countless short stories daily and then, when sound arrived in 1927, desperately needed even more writers to supply lots of talk. (Even in the Depression, MGM would release a full-length film every week). Scott Fitzgerald was clearly speaking from experience when in one exchange in *The Last Tycoon*, the protagonist, a studio boss named Monroe Stahr, modeled on MGM's legendary young production chief, Irving Thalberg, describes the schizophrenic love/hate relationship that existed between the people who made the movies and the talents that wrote them.

> *"We don't have good writers out here."* [Says Stahr to a visitor early in the novel.]
> *"Why you can hire anyone!"* exclaimed his visitor in surprise.
> *"Oh we hire them but when they get out here they're not good writers—so we have to work with the material we have."*
> *"Like what?"*
> *"Anybody that'll accept the system and stay decently sober—we have all sorts of people—disappointed poets, one-hit playwrights, college girls—we put them on an idea in pairs and if it*

slows down we put two more writers working behind them. I've had as many as three pairs working on the same idea."

"Do they like that?"

"Not if they know about it. They're not geniuses—none of them could make as much any other way."

Novelist Budd (*On the Waterfront*) Schulberg, whose father, B. P. Schulberg, ran Paramount from 1926 until 1932, was one of those who contributed mightily to Fitzgerald's posthumous Hollywood reputation as a broken-down, drunken failure. His 1950 novel, *The Disenchanted*, described Manley Halliday's (Fitzgerald's stand-in) ten-day binge when he and the twenty-four-year old Schulberg visited a snowy Dartmouth College in February 1939, researching the upcoming Walter Wanger film *Winter Carnival*. Schulberg, for whom Fitzgerald had little respect and whom Fitzgerald once described as "Budd, the untalented," was kinder to Fitzgerald's memory at a USC centenary symposium when he explained that unlike most writers, Fitzgerald actually liked Hollywood and used the industry as a great literary resource in his final novel.

"Scott had great dreams about Hollywood," Schulberg said. "It was not just the money. Most of the writers I knew—Faulkner and the others—just wanted to get the money and get out. Scott was different. He believed in the movies. He thought it was a great medium, and he thought it was one that any writer had to know, to learn. He thought it was the storytelling of the future, and he admired the moviemaker, as you can see from the remarkable vigor he had in portraying Monroe Stahr in *The Last Tycoon*."

Fitzgerald also upset Schulberg by using him and his anecdotes about Hollywood in the novel:

"When Scott showed me the opening chapter of *The Last Tycoon* and I read the opening paragraph and scanned the first page," Schulberg also reminisced at USC, "I have to confess that my feelings were hurt. The book had opened with—well, there was an odd feeling of reading my own words, as I had said to Scott that, being raised in Hollywood, there didn't seem to be anything glamorous about it. It was a town that turned out a product. Instead of automobiles or tires or steel, in our town we turned out cans of film. And we had to turn out so many a week to keep the wheels turning. I said we live in a company town, just as much a company town as any coal town in West Virginia. And it's about that glamorous. That was all there, and I thought, 'Gee, I thought Scott really liked me, but I guess I was just something that came along that was very handy for him.'

"Scott saw the look on my face. He was one of the gentlest, kindest, most sympathetic and generous writers I've ever met. At the same time, of course, he couldn't stop lifting something somebody else said, because that's the profession he was in. He looked at me and said, 'Yes, Budd, I guess in Cecelia (the narrator of *The Last Tycoon*, a film magnate's daughter sharing the name of Cecil B. DeMille's daughter) I did combine you with Scottie (Fitzgerald's daughter).'"

Of course, Fitzgerald and dozens of other high-profile writers such as Nunnally Johnson, James Agee, and Aldous Huxley were a class apart from the "schmucks with Underwoods," as Jack Warner once described the writers whom he stabled in tiny cubicles (called rabbit warrens) in the worst buildings on his lot. Writers like Fitzgerald were often treated like literary royalty, with a commensurate income. This was not always the case, of course. William Faulkner's salary during his Hollywood years when he was, ironically, working at Warner Brothers, was three hundred dollars a week, and he wore his desperation publicly. Although he felt either above writing screenplays or unsure he had the talent to write them (probably a little of both), Faulkner, in financial straits, once offered his services to anyone who would pay him more than a hundred dollars a week. Soon after arriving in Hollywood in 1941, Bertolt Brecht also realized the only way for a writer to survive in the film capital was to, of course, sell out and write films (he never did), and he penned the following bittersweet ditty:

> Every morning to earn my bread,
> I go to the market, where lies are bought.
> Hopefully
> I join the ranks of the sellers.

Although the $1250 a week Fitzgerald received in 1938 put him in the top 15 percent of earners, and his portrayal of the high life of Hollywood in *The Last Tycoon* has blurred the memory of his Hollywood output, he, also wrote about the plight of the screen-writing "hacks." A series of seventeen short stories he wrote for magazines introduced a mediocre writer named Pat Hobby who started as a writer of titles in silent films and evolved into a writer of screenplays in the 1930s.

For all of his disdain for Hollywood, William Faulkner did manage to have his name attached to more films than Fitzgerald did. Some of them were the usual pap, but two of them from his last stay in the film capital are classics: 1944's *To Have and Have Not* and 1946's *The Big Sleep*. Both were directed by the famous comedy and action writer/director Howard Hawks, and both starred Humphrey Bogart and Lauren Bacall. (Bacall's familiar directions to Bogart in *To Have and Have Not* on how to whistle for her—

"You just put your lips together and blow"—was actually written for Bacall's screen test by Hawks; it was Faulkner's challenge to write a scene around that line for the movie). Both Faulkner and veteran screenwriter Jules Furthman's collaboration with Hawks on *To Have and Have Not* was partially to fulfill a bet between Ernest Hemingway and Hawks that it would be impossible for the director to make a successful film out of what is generally accepted as Hemingway's poorest novel.

Faulkner, like Fitzgerald, first came to Hollywood in 1932 to mine the film capital's gold. His last hope for money from his books died when the publisher of his fifth novel, *Sanctuary*, went bankrupt six months after the book's publication in 1931. In fact, the only money to come from *Sanctuary* came from the sale of its film rights to Paramount and, because of his notoriety, a screenwriting contract from MGM.

The casual atmosphere of Hollywood still irritates many today; in the far more formal 1930s it was even more of an issue. But the perceived stuffiness of easterners irritated Southern Californians as well, and such it was with the film colony's general response to the diminutive (five-foot) Faulkner, always impeccably dressed in his signature, sometimes worn, tweeds. But it wasn't his clothes that were the problem; it was his low-pitched Mississippi drawl that made him literally unintelligible to many fellow workers, as well as his famous reserve that came off, more often than not, as a sort of elitist rudeness. And, of course, there was Faulkner's legendary drinking, which easily rivaled Fitzgerald's at its most outrageous.

One problem with many good anecdotes about Hollywood is that after they make the rounds, everyone tries to claim them for their own. Such is the case of the most famous story about Faulkner's time in Hollywood—the "I'm working at home" incident. Although

Jack Warner later claimed the incident took place at his studio in the 1940s, and at least one film historian places it at Twentieth Century Fox in the late 1930s, Faulkner's now legendary response to a studio clerk's query actually happened in 1932 when he was working on a script at MGM for Howard Hawks called *Today We Live*. (Hawks thought Faulkner would be expert at writing the clipped sort of British dialogue he wanted in the film, but his work turned out to be more of a caricature.)

While working on *Today We Live*, a mushy, World War I romance drama starring Robert Young, Gary Cooper, and Joan Crawford (whose last-minute availability to make the film caused a complete rewrite of the script), Faulkner's father suddenly died. He returned home to Oxford, Mississippi and continued working on the script via telephone with the clear understanding from Hawks that he could do so. When the script was finished, Hawks and Faulkner agreed to continue their association and the (now six-hundred-dollar) weekly paychecks continued as well as the understanding that he could continue working "at home." That is, until a clerk at the studio tried to reach the author and discovered that when Faulkner said he was "working at home," not an unusual working arrangement in Hollywood then or now, he meant he was working two thousand miles away, which definitely *was* unusual. When it was discovered, Faulkner was ordered to immediately join the New Orleans location shoot for the studio's *Lazy River* and then, after three weeks, fired. Subsequently, the studio wired him that he was always welcome to join the staff in California.

It wasn't long before Faulkner was back out in Hollywood for a short stay, working in mid-1934 on another Hawks project (this time for Universal) called *Sutter's Gold*; the movie went nowhere, but the stay apparently produced his only story about Hollywood, "The Golden Land," in which he described Hollywood as a place of "almost incalculable wealth" whose "queerly appropriate fate it is to be erected upon a few spools of substance whose value is computed in billions and which may be completely destroyed [by] a careless match." In November of the following year, Faulkner returned to Hollywood to crank out—as was his habit when working on a screenplay that he regarded simply as a job to get done as fast as possible—an astonishing thirty-five pages a day for Twentieth Century Fox's *The Road to Glory*. Other than for a few visits home, he remained in the film capital for nearly two years, receiving a "story by William Faulkner" credit on a film named *Slave Ship* that he, in fact, didn't write (it was based on a novel). When asked about this, he said much about the work he did at the time: "I'm a motion picture doctor. When they run into a section they don't like, I rework it and continue to rework it until they do like it. I don't write scripts. I don't know enough about it."

Like many other high-profile writers in Hollywood, including John O'Hara, Erskine Caldwell, Dashiell Hammett, Gene Fowler, and Scott Fitzgerald, Faulkner was a familiar face at the bookstore of a self-proclaimed "con man" named Stanley Rose who was an intimate of many local drug dealers, gangsters, and pimps. Located on Hollywood Boulevard near Musso and Frank's, whose bar was a favorite writer's hangout, the bookstore even had slot machines in the back. Rose, who later became a literary agent representing, among others, William Saroyan, was memorialized by Faulkner's occasional hunting partner Nathanael West in *The Day of the Locust* via the use of his name on the business card of the dwarf Honest Abe Kusich.

By 1942 Faulkner's finances were in such terrible shape that he was begging his literary agent for some sort of advance, claiming he didn't even have fifteen dollars to pay his electricity bill. The contract he was finally able to wangle out of Warner Brothers guaranteed the forty-five-year-old writer only a "junior writer's" three hundred dollars weekly (out of which two agents' commissions also had to be paid). The thirty-nine months he spent in Hollywood (July 1942 to September 1945) were difficult (wartime rationing of everything from gasoline to food certainly didn't help) and humiliating (his Random House royalties from *all* his books amounted to only three hundred dollars in 1942; he was in bondage to Hollywood whether he liked it or not).

In the fall of 1945, after having worked on sixteen screenplays, most of which were never produced, Faulkner left the film capital for the penultimate time; he would return for eight weeks in 1951 to write the script for William Barrett's religious novel *The Left Hand of God*, which was never filmed. In 1953 and 1954, he travelled to Europe and Egypt to collaborate on the script for Hawks's DeMille-like spectacular, *The Land of the Pharaohs*. In 1955 and again in 1958, Faulkner turned down lucrative offers to write the screenplays for several of his novels, telling his agent: "I am no good at picture scripts, and I had better leave this alone and stick to my own work."

When Faulkner left Hollywood, he took with him an agreement about a project that would more or less constitute his "own work" for the rest of his life. At the end of 1943, producer William Bacher and director Henry Hathaway, whose 1952 film *Niagara* put Marilyn Monroe on Hollywood's map, formed a partnership with Faulkner to develop a film based on the popularity of World War I's Unknown Soldier legend. It would result in Faulkner's longest and possibly worst novel, *A Fable,* published in 1954.

Faulkner always seemed angry about California because he knew he was bound to it for economic reasons. He often referred to it as "that damned West Coast place" and famously once described life in Southern California this way: "Nothin' ever happens an' after a while a couple of leaves fall off a tree and then it'll be another year. I don't like the climate, the people, their way of life."

Anita Loos loved Hollywood, and it doesn't take a psychology degree to suspect that was one reason the film community took to her and not to Faulkner nearly a decade after she wrote *Gentlemen Prefer Blondes*, a novel that Winston Churchill kept on his bedside table and James Joyce spent hours reading even when he was losing his eyesight.

Born in Sissons (now Mount Shasta), California, in 1893, Loos arrived in Hollywood early, writing more than a hundred half-hour slapstick comedies for, among several silent film directors, D. W. Griffith. Her first produced movie was the *The New York Hat*, directed by Griffith in 1912 and starring Mary Pickford, Lionel Barrymore and Lillian and Dorothy Gish; it was a one-reeler for which she was paid twenty-five dollars. Before moving to New York with her actor/director husband John Emerson to, as she wrote, "escape the kooks, weirdos, and incompetents who . . . created (Hollywood's) cultural atmospheres," Loos would write the titles for the great director's magnum opus, 1916's *Intolerance*, borrowing the line for one of them from Voltaire ("When women cease to attract men, they take to noble deeds to attract attention"). "In those thoughtless days," she later said, "none of us ever associated movies with art; such 'easy money' placed them in the category of striking oil."

In 1924 Loos struck a gusher when she wrote a story poking fun at a romance the writer and humorist H. L. Mencken was having with "a stupid little blonde." Within a year the spoof would be published, first as a serial in *Harper's Bazaar*; then it would begin a run through eighty-five editions as a book and be made into a 1928 movie, a Broadway musical (with songs by Jule Styne), and a 1953 movie of the musical starring Jane Russell and Marilyn Monroe. Loos called it *Gentlemen Prefer Blondes*.

Success breeds success, so it is no surprise that by the end of 1931, Loos was on her way back to Hollywood and to MGM, where she would remain for the next eighteen years. Irving Thalberg's offer of $3500 weekly was too good to turn down; the erosion of her marriage was another reason to move on, too. She was to write—actually to rewrite, as she discovered in her first meeting with the studio's production chief—the script Fitzgerald and a cowriter he hated could get nowhere with, *Red-Headed Woman*, a project to star a henna-wigged Jean Harlow. In their first meeting, Thalberg explained why he wanted her on the project, putting his finger on Loos's major appeal for Hollywood; what he received from Fitzgerald was a "tome poem," he said. What he needed was to have the sex element in the soap opera–like novel by Katherine Brush made fun of . . . "just as . . . [Loos] did in *Gentlemen Prefer Blondes*."

Years later Loos elaborated: "To Irving Thalberg every film had to be a love story. . . . It wasn't necessary at all for the affair to concern people of the opposite sex. . . . Furthermore, age had nothing to do with the matter. One of Irving's [Thalberg's] most poignant screen romances was *The Champ*, in which the relationship between Jackie Cooper (aged six) and Wallace Beery (a grizzled sixty) held all the rapture of a love affair. And in *Mutiny on the Bounty* starring Clark Gable and Charles Laughton (1935), there would be a rivalry so bitter it could only have been based on the strongest mutual fascination."

Red-Headed Woman made Jean Harlow a superstar, but despite the rumor that the British royal family kept a copy at Buckingham

Palace to entertain guests after dinner, the film made history by bringing on stringent censorship that would cause difficulties for the industry for years to come. It happened not because Harlow's character—a secretary who cold-bloodedly schemes to break up her boss's marriage—was salacious, but because she got away with it, ending up rich, happy, and respected.

From then on, Loos's career was one triumph after another: the late-night television staple *San Francisco* in 1936, *Saratoga* the following year (during the making of which Jean Harlow became ill and died of uremia; her part was completed by a stand-in wearing a platinum wig and shot from behind), and, in 1939 shared screenwriting credits with Jane Murfin on *The Women,* the film version of Clare Boothe Luce's then-daring venomous satire with an all-female cast including Norma Shearer, Rosalind Russell, Paulette Goddard, and Joan Crawford.

Mencken once told Anita Loos: "Do you realize, young woman, that you're the first American writer ever to poke fun at sex?" In her old age, the writer bitterly criticized the crassness with which sex was exploited in Hollywood. "And if we have to tell Hollywood good-bye," Anita Loos wrote not long before her death at eighty in 1971, "it may be with one of those tender, old-fashioned, seven-second kisses exchanged between two people of the *opposite* sex, with all their clothes on."

That viewpoint may be unfashionable among many in Hollywood today, but at least Loos, who could dish up scandalous asides and one-liners with the best of them, stayed popular with most of the film colony.

Not so for another famous female wit. Poet, short-story writer, drama critic (for the original *Vanity Fair*), and screenwriter Dorothy Parker of the Algonquin Round Table fame is remembered today less for her screenplays (including 1937's *A*

Star Is Born, for which she shared the screenwriting Oscar with her second husband, Alan Campbell, and Robert Carson) than for aiming one-liners at people and institutions with the accuracy of a laser-guided missile. Remember "Men don't make passes at girls who wear glasses"? She hated that line and the fame it brought her, always believing that people admired her talent for the wrong reason. Never one to turn down a drink, after moving to Hollywood in 1933, she and Campbell seemingly spent more time falling off barstools in pubs near their bungalow at 8933 Norma Place in West Hollywood than actually working. Nevertheless, Parker ended up with fifteen screen credits to her name and was instrumental in forming the Screen Writers Guild with Lillian Hellman and her common-law husband, Dashiell Hammett. Both of Parker's husbands died with drugs in their blood, and she attempted suicide at least four times:

> *Razors pain you*
> *Rivers are damp*
> *Acid stains you*
> *And drugs give cramp.*
> *Guns aren't lawful*
> *Nooses give*
> *Gas smells awful*
> *You might as well live.*

Nevertheless, it wasn't Parker's alcoholism that finally turned Hollywood against her, but her habit of biting the hand that fed her with barbs such as her 1934 review of a stage performance of Katharine Hepburn's ("running the gamut from A to B") and her outspoken leftist politics in an era that was marked with near hysterical anticommunism. Still, Parker somehow survived in Hollywood for thirty years before returning to New York in 1963.

After her death in New York in 1967, Parker was cremated, and then, it seems, everyone forgot what to do with her ashes, a circumstance Dorothy Parker might have bitterly relished. Lillian Hellman was Parker's executor and, after making the funeral arrangements, neglected—deliberately or otherwise, as she was in a pitched battle for Parker's inheritance—to tell the funeral home what to do with the ashes. So, after sitting on a shelf for six years, they were mailed to her former lawyers' office. There they sat in a file cabinet for another fifteen years until in 1988 it was suddenly discovered the ashes were still unclaimed. The NAACP, to whom (over Hellman's loud objections) Parker had left what little money she had when she died, claimed them at last and placed them in a memorial garden in the organization's Baltimore headquarters. Sadly, the marker does not read, as Dorothy Parker once requested, "Excuse My Dust."

In the early 1930s, MGM's Billy Haines was one of the hottest stars in Hollywood . . . and then it ended overnight. Haines's downfall wasn't due to the fact that he was gay, though Haines did flaunt his sexuality. But he also had the last laugh—after studio boss Louis B. Mayer fired him, friends, including Joan Crawford and Carole Lombard, helped him build a decorating business that made him a millionaire.

"Twilight" Guys and Gals

In the 1920s and 1930s, Hollywood was probably one of the most gay-friendly cities in the world.

It was a place where relationships between "twilight" men and women (as they were called at the time), such as that between Cary Grant and Randolph Scott (yes, read on), Greta Garbo and Mercedes de Acosta, and Marlene Dietrich and Claudette Colbert were accepted as part of the social landscape. Although the patrons of Jimmy's Backyard, Hollywood's first gay bar ("pansy club" was the term, then somewhat less pejorative than now), which opened on New Year's Eve, 1929, were exclusively homosexual, both gays and straights patronized most of the others, including B.B.B.'s Cellar, which featured a famous drag show, and the Friendship bar in Santa Monica, where straight-arrow Will Rogers, who lived nearby, often showed up. Such openness would be forced into the closet in 1934 when Hollywood's self-censoring Film

Production Code, toeing the line of the Catholic bishops' Legion of Decency, forbade the depiction of homosexuality in any form.

Such a gay-friendly atmosphere in the early days—again evident in Hollywood even after years of media and police homophobia—was inevitable. The film capital has always been home to a greater percentage of gays and lesbians than has the rest of the country; it went with the territory, where set and costume designers, makeup artists, and actors and actresses as well as screenwriters, were in constant demand.

The studio chiefs during Hollywood's golden years knew and accepted this even if they were, like Louis B. Mayer, homophobic—after all, they had to make movies. But they did everything they could to mask the reality from the ticket-buying public. The news that their high-priced romantic hero might be gay was box-office death in Middle America. And if that meant sacrificing a big star who got caught publicly in an embarrassing situation with a companion of the same gender—well, business has always been business in Hollywood.

Most stars were complicit in keeping their true sexuality hidden from their fans. But the gossip-driven linking of Cary Grant—one of the best and most popular actors in the history of film—with Randolph Scott was exactly what it seemed to be. For years (and during four unhappy marriages) Grant assumed, in the eyes of his younger fans, the image of a witty urbane, and completely heterosexual star who once shared a "bachelor pad" in Santa Monica and an apartment in Hollywood with Scott between each star's marriages. Sure.

In the 1970s Grant even sued Chevy Chase, then a cast member of *Saturday Night Live*, for referring to him on air as a "homo." But facts are facts. Until he had to make the choice between his profession and his sexual orientation in the early 1930s, it never bothered Cary Grant to spend his time more or less exclusively in the company of gay men. In 1921 and recently arrived from England, the seventeen-year-old vaudeville acrobat named Archie Leach—the Cary Grant moniker arrived later—roomed with two gay friends in Greenwich Village. One of them was said to be his lover: a twenty-three-year-old Australian painter named Jack Kelly, later famous in Hollywood as an Oscar-winning costume designer who used the stage name Orry-Kelly.

In 1932, Leach moved to Hollywood along with Orry-Kelly and fell in love with the ruggedly handsome Scott, once said to have been Howard Hughes's boyfriend. They immediately set up housekeeping together at 2177 West Live Oak Drive in the Los Feliz district adjacent to Hollywood. The relationship was so well known in the film community that the press referred to them as the "happy couple," and radio gossip columnist Jimmy Fiedler once sniped: "These guys are carrying the buddy business a bit too far." Actress Carole Lombard was quoted in the *Los Angeles Times* as saying: "I wonder which of those two guys pays the bills?" Apart from a series of studio "at home" pictures of the then inseparable Grant and Scott at their beach house in Santa Monica that rang every contemporary gay or at least effete stereotype—pinkie ring on Scott, a poodle, etc.—there is also a lot of direct testimony from such people as Orry-Kelly, friends such as George Burns and George Cukor, and Grant's secretary, Frank Horn, that supports the truth of the relationship. Despite the fact that William Randolph Hearst and Marion Davies "lived in sin" for decades, there was a hard and fast rule that couples invited to weekend at Hearst's San Simeon palace had to be married. It was rarely broken for any couple, gay or straight, except frequent guests Cary Grant and Randolph Scott. And, although the heterosexual Mae West preferred muscle-bound hunks in the sack, many of her male film costars were gay. And who were the costars in three of her biggest films? Cary Grant in *She Done Him Wrong* and *I'm No Angel*, and Randolph Scott in *Go West Young Man*.

And Gary Cooper? Although he had affairs with such female stars as the "It" girl herself, Clara Bow, and the "Mexican spitfire" Lupe Velez, a cousin of the openly gay young Paramount contract player Anderson Lawler claims that Lawler and Cooper were lovers, lived together for a time in 1929, and that "Coop" also had an affair with *Vanity Fair* photographer Cecil Beaton, himself later a highly visible companion of the sexually equivocal Greta Garbo.

Because of the rapidly shifting moral standards of the 1930s, Paramount pressured both Grant and Scott into marriages: Grant, in February 1934, to the shy actress Virginia Cherrill who played opposite Charlie Chaplin in *City Lights*; and Scott to Marianna duPont in 1936. In fact, Grant was so unhappy in his marriage to Cherrill that he began drinking heavily (which continued through his four subsequent marriages to Barbara Hutton, Betsy Drake, Dyan Cannon, and Barbara Harris), became surly (which also continued in private), and attempted suicide. As for Scott, he never lived with duPont. After having his stomach pumped, Grant moved back in with Scott in the apartment conveniently situated next door to the one Grant and Cherrill "shared" in West Hollywood's still-standing La Ronda Apartments. The pair continued to live together off and on until 1942. Grant would later say of this time: "I pretended to be somebody I wanted to be, and finally I became that person."

Humor—at least black humor—has always been part of the gay persona, probably originating as a defense mechanism for combating ages of verbal abuse, social profiling, as well as active persecution. A perfect example is the tale of the accidental death of the German film director F. W. Murnau, who arrived in Hollywood in

1927. As tragic as the story is, I've never found any gay person (and few straight ones) who didn't think it was one of the most morbidly funny yarns from the early days of Hollywood.

Murnau, forty-two, then famous as "the German D. W. Griffith" for making such films as the campily creepy *Nosferatu* (1922), 1925's *The Last Laugh* (starring Emil Jennings), and his 1929 masterpiece, *Sunrise,* had a reputation—like Valentino's lesbian friend Alla Nazimova—for casting his films more or less solely with gay actors such as *Sunrise's* Janet Gaynor.

On March 11, 1931, not long after Murnau's return from Tahiti, where he filmed *Tabu,* the director, a fourteen-year-old Filipino named Garcia Stevenson with whom he was carrying on a torrid affair, Ned Martin, manager of the sound company that synchronized *Tabu,* Murnau's German shepherd, Pal, and chauffeur John Freeland were driving north from Los Angeles in a rented Packard. They were bound for Carmel to meet the writer William Morris about writing a book based on the film. During a gas stop at the Rio Grande Oil Station in Elwood, twelve miles before Santa Barbara, Garcia took the wheel at Murnau's request and the chauffer got in the backseat.

They only got five miles before the Packard swerved off the road and crashed to the bottom of an embankment. Everyone escaped with minor injuries except Murnau, who was fatally injured and died that night in a Santa Barbara hospital. The story that instantly circulated like wildfire in Hollywood claimed Murnau was crushed by the steering wheel beneath which he was crouched at the time of the accident, performing fellatio on Stevenson and that his subsequent orgasm caused Stevenson to lose control of the car. Because of the scandal, only eleven people showed up at Murnau's funeral at Pierce Brothers Mortuary. But one of them was his friend Greta Garbo, who ordered a death mask of the director before his casket was sealed and shipped back to Germany; Garbo kept it on her desk for all of the years she lived in Hollywood.

Murnau met his death at the feet of a boy who very likely was, at least when they met, a hired hustler. There is no question, however, that it was a pair of ruthless hustlers who were responsible for the 1968 death of Ramon Novarro, in his time one of the most popular and openly gay actors in Hollywood. Novarro's murder still ranks as one of the grisliest in Hollywood's history.

Born Jose Ramón Gil Samaniegos in Durango, Mexico, in 1899, Novarro came to Los Angeles in 1913. He grocery-clerked, ushered, and dreamed of an operatic career while working as a busboy at the then elegant Alexandria Hotel (where he met and became a lover and close friend of Valentino, then breaking into films as a dancer).

It wasn't long before Ramon's sultry Latin looks caught the attention of director Rex Ingram, once hailed by the director and actor Erich von Stroheim as "the world's greatest director," who cast him as an extra in a number of films including Valentino's great breakthrough movie, 1921's *The Four Horsemen of the Apocalypse*. After Valentino jumped to Paramount, Novarro became Metro's male-siren when he was cast as the star of Ingram's *The Prisoner of Zenda*, and, in 1923, as the swashbuckler Scaramouche in the first film version of Rafael Sabatini's hugely successful novel (his *Zenda* salary, $125 weekly, was increased over the next two years to $10,000, the equivalent of $150,000 *a week* in today's money). To celebrate his younger friend's success, Valentino gave him a lead, Art Deco–style phallic symbol (also a sly reference to their earlier relationship and their mutual fame as sex symbols) with his signature inlaid in silver. Then, cast as Ben-Hur in the MGM's lavish, 1926 biblical adventure—the first and in many ways the best version of the story remade in 1959 with Charlton Heston in his role—Novarro became a superstar. The following year, MGM production chief Irving Thalberg cast Novarro opposite his new wife, Norma Shearer, in a no-cost-spared production of *The Student Prince,* directed by Ernst Lubitsch. Like *Ben-Hur,* it remains a classic of the silent era.

Although he also made the transition into sound fairly successfully when he sang the soon popular "Pagan Love Song" to Renée Adorée in 1930's *The Pagan* (in which, presumably to titillate his millions of female admirers, Novarro wore the scantiest clothes the censor would allow), it was his *singing* voice the public seemed to like, not his speaking voice. Despite a wonderful performance opposite Greta Garbo in 1931's *Mata Hari,* Novarro had somehow lost his following, and three years later, MGM tore up his contract.

He withdrew to his ranch near San Diego, drowned his frustration in alcohol, and for a time even contemplated entering a Trappist monastery after the Jesuit order turned him down for "being too old" to join the order. Despite a couple of foreign films and a pair for Republic, Novarro more or less retired to his Lloyd Wright–designed house in the Hollywood Hills (later owned by actress Diane Keaton) and wasn't seen on the screen again until he appeared as a character actor in four films in 1949; then he disappeared again. Novarro only reemerged in 1960 for a cameo role in George Cukor's *Heller in Pink Tights* and eventually transitioned to television via character appearances in such shows as *Bonanza* and *Dr. Kildare* before permanently retiring behind the rustic walls of his last home at 3110 Laurel Canyon Boulevard. As age and weight eroded his once stunning looks, he sought the company of hustlers; after his death, 140 checks were found written to male prostitutes during one six-month period.

And then came the Halloween eve of October 30, 1968, when Paul Ferguson, a twenty-three-year-old James Dean look-alike from Chicago who had been twice convicted for assault with a deadly weapon and served time in Wyoming for grand theft, and his seventeen-year-old brother, Tom, rang Novarro's doorbell.

Apparently, either both Ferguson brothers had heard from other hustlers that Novarro had five thousand dollars hidden in the house or Paul, whom the actor had apparently been seeing for a few weeks, had heard of the stash; in any event, they probably planned to rob Novarro for drug money. After arriving at his house, demanding cigarettes (Novarro had a carton delivered from a local drugstore), and drinking a lot (the garbage can was filled with empty liquor bottles), Novarro and Paul Ferguson disappeared into the star's bedroom after the actor called his agent to set up a meeting to help both brothers break into films.

Tom then called his girlfriend in Chicago to tell her about the potential career break, talking for some forty-five minutes, until he heard screams from the bedroom and hung up, explaining, "I don't want Paul to hurt Ramon." After grabbing a couple of beers, he went to the bedroom, where he discovered the nude, semiconscious Novarro covered with blood and Paul standing by the bed, his white shorts also bloodstained. After dragging the actor into the shower to clean him up, the pair put him back on the bed; Paul then raided Novarro's closet, adorning himself in a black vest and fedora and doing a dance in front of a mirror, twirling Novarro's ivory-tipped cane while the actor murmured Hail Marys. When Novarro somehow pulled himself to his feet, Paul beat him nearly to death with the cane.

The pair then ransacked the house for the rumored five thousand dollars (but found only forty-five) and, at Tom's suggestion to make the crime look like a robbery or rape, tied the actor's hands behind his back with the cord from the bedside light, strewed condoms around the room, scratched the actor's back with a knife to make it appear he had been wounded by a woman's nails, and scribbled "Us girls are better than fagits" on the mirror in the now blood-soaked room.

It is not true, as was widely gossiped at the time, that Novarro's genitals had been cut off and shoved down his throat. But the lead phallus given him by Valentino all those years earlier apparently *had* been shoved in his mouth, causing the actor to choke to death on his own blood. Before hitching a ride back down to Sunset Boulevard, Paul broke the cane and placed its ivory tip between Novarro's legs, and on the way out, he threw his own bloody underwear over the fence.

The brothers Ferguson were easily caught; police checked the phone records, called Tom's girlfriend, and got the whole story. After their arrest, Paul convinced Tom to confess to the crime since as a juvenile, he would face only a year in jail and would provide an accomplice for his brother, so Paul would avoid the gas chamber. When the court agreed that Tom could be tried as an adult, he immediately recanted his confession, and during the trial, each accused the other of torturing and killing the actor. Each was convicted of the murder, sentenced to life in prison but released on parole after only seven years.

After his release, Tom, who would be only 52 today, disappeared. Not so Paul. He moved to Doniphan, Missouri, where he ran a successful rodeo promotion and construction business for several years, often boasting of having been a model convict at San Quentin. In 1989 Paul Ferguson was again arrested, tried, and convicted on a rape charge and sentenced to sixty years in prison. While out on appeal he was convicted of rape in another state and is presently serving two consecutive thirty-year terms for rape and sodomy at the Missouri Eastern Correctional Center in Pacific, Missouri. He will be eligible for his first parole hearing in 2008.

Like Novarro, another famous director may have died at the hands of a hustler. After directing such classics as 1931's *Frankenstein, The Bride of Frankenstein* (1935), and 1939's *The Man in the Iron Mask* for Universal, the British-born James Whale retired to his Pacific Palisades mansion when his fondness for young men became too public. But, despite the tale retold in the recent film *Gods and Monsters*, which starred the openly gay actor Ian McKellen as Whale, when the director was found dead in his pool in 1957, many were convinced— a subsequently discovered suicide note notwithstanding—that he was killed by a hustler he had hired to pose nude for a portrait. Whale had taken up painting after he "retired" from films.

The fate of some gay actors in the golden age was kinder; certainly so in the case of William Haines, popular star of the late 1920s and early 1930s. Haines not only survived the loss of his career because of his sexual orientation; he and his lover also survived one of the most highly publicized cases of gay bashing in the 1930s. For much of his decade-long career, Billy Haines was typecast as a character that is inseparable from the popular image of the Jazz Age itself—a breezy, wisecracking charmer who made a half dozen films a year at MGM, starring opposite such talent as Joan Crawford, Marion Davies (in 1928's *Show People,* an endearingly charming film directed by King Vidor), and Mary Pickford.

In 1933, all that came to an abrupt end when, apparently after he was caught in flagrante delicto with a young sailor at the downtown Los Angeles YMCA, Louis B. Mayer, who had earlier told his handsome leading man to ditch his longtime lover Jimmy Shields and get married, instantly fired his leading "fegeleh." Haines immediately turned to decorating and to his earlier, largely straight, costars. With the support of such friends as Joan Crawford (for whom he created her trademark all-white decor), Marion Davies, and Carole Lombard (whose home was his first big commission), Haines became Hollywood's most successful decorator to the stars and eventually for many others. He also designed Jack Warner's palatial home (sadly gutted by its new owner, David Geffen) and, in 1965, decorated the Palm Springs home of *TV Guide* founder Walter Annenberg and wife, Lee. Five years later, he designed highly publicized million-dollar redo of Winfield House, the U.S. ambassador's official residence in London, after President Nixon appointed Annenberg to the prestigious station.

Haines is also the apparent key to the explanation for the once puzzling replacement of *Gone with the Wind*'s original director, George Cukor, by Victor Fleming in 1939—certainly the most famous directorial change in film history. Although some deny it, the legend claims that years earlier, when Clark Gable was working as an extra in one of Haines's films, Cukor had a sexual encounter with the star. Years later, Gable, terrified that Haines may have told Cukor—who was a friend of Haines and also gay—about the encounter (he in fact had), demanded the director's replacement by his friend Fleming ("a man's director"). The producer, David Selznick, himself frustrated over creative differences with Cukor, was happy to accommodate his star, even over the protests of his leading lady, Vivien Leigh.

Gay bashing was very much present in Hollywood in the beginning of the twentieth century. In 1936, Haines, Shields, and their poodle (dyed purple for Easter) were beaten up by the White Legion, a Southern California version of the KKK. It happened near their beach house in the El Porto part of Manhattan

Beach after a rumor started that Shields had molested six-year-old Jimmy Walker, the son of a local businessman. No charges were ever filed for lack of evidence, but the scandal made headlines across America.

Haines's acting career lasted fourteen years. His decorating career lasted some forty years and made him a multimillionaire. Living well was certainly Billy Haines's best revenge.

Haines was also close to Claudette Colbert, who, with costar Clark Gable, won an Oscar for her performance in Frank Capra's 1934 classic *It Happened One Night*. Although she never told Haines that she was a lesbian or that she and Marlene Dietrich, frequent guests of Haines and Shield's palatial home at 1712 Stanley in Hollywood, were lovers (that had to wait until the death of Colbert's second husband, Dr. Joel Pressman), she very definitely and happily was gay. But, like Cary Grant and Randolph Scott, she was also forced by Paramount to marry, and although she did so, the couple divorced in 1935 at about the time Colbert started her relationship with Dietrich. Like the Grant/Scott relationship, the Colbert/Dietrich affair was also fairly public, far too public, in fact, for the times; Paramount was highly embarrassed by a widely circulated photo of both wearing pants—then a code for lesbianism created by Greta Garbo and her lover, Mercedes de Acosta—careening down a slide together at a party given by Carole Lombard. In short order Colbert married Pressman and Dietrich began her torrid relationship with John Gilbert, who within a year would drink himself to death.

Some actresses may have been so hidden in the closet that we'll never even suspect, but, although Barbara Stanwyck was married to

Robert Taylor, one of the most handsome actors in Hollywood (and always dogged by rumors of homosexuality; he once begged Louis B. Mayer to cast him in more rugged, he-man roles), she was considered by many to be the most famous closeted lesbian in Hollywood. Her comment when once challenged about her preferences? "I admire the girls who never married. Me, I wouldn't have the guts." Many also believe that the highly publicized Stanwyck/Taylor marriage in 1939 was nothing more than a studio-managed way of quenching the rumors, and Taylor eventually married the much younger Ursula Thiess. On the other hand, some actresses such as the much loved Spring Byington didn't bother with covering up their true nature; Byington openly admitted her relationship with the character actress Marjorie Main, who said of her (Main's) famous character, Ma Kettle: "She was the real man in the house."

Hollywood has always dealt in clichés, after all; a cliché is usually a more comforting way to tell a story than by recounting the facts. And one cliché is that while many of the silent-era scenario writers (like DeMille's Jennie McPherson, Valentino's first wife, Jean Acker, and the ubiquitous Salka Viertel, probably Garbo's closest Hollywood friend and the writer of her 1933 film *Queen Christina*, with its celebrated woman/woman kiss) were lesbians, most of the female stars (with such obvious exceptions as Alla Nazimova) were as straight as a razor blade. Not so: In fact, "Gillette" was often a word used to describe the sexual preference of many of them; like the double-edged blade, it cut both ways. Often, as did Janet Gaynor, Lili Damita, Agnes Morehead, Elsa Lancester, Joan Crawford, and Judy Garland (to name just a few of the lesbian and bisexual female actors making up what author Axel Madsen has termed "daisy chains of deceit"), they got married—often to gay or bisexual men—and occasionally had children. Gaynor wed the gay MGM costume designer Adrian; Damita married Errol Flynn, who, despite his reputation for womanizing, occasionally played with boys; Morehead, especially popular in later life as the witch Endora on TV's *Bewitched,* married the twenty-years-younger Robert Gist—the marriage lasted less than a year; Lancester married the closeted gay Charles Laughton; and Crawford even made a pass at a hired nurse ("She'd sleep with a squirrel," remarked one Hollywood friend). This sort of cover-up still continues. Sandy Dennis always maintained that she was married to jazz musician Gerry Mulligan; however, after her death in 1992, *People* magazine searched in vain for legal evidence of the marriage.

Although at the time there wasn't any question about Murnau's or Haines's sexual orientation (nor, for that matter, about that of later—and more careful—stars such as Clifton Webb and Tyrone Power and musician Cole Porter), when it came to major gay or bisexual film stars, unless they appeared clearly heterosexual, the truth was always (and largely still is) masked. Posterity has thus inherited a "were they or weren't they" question that still surrounds such stars as Rudolph Valentino (he was bisexual).

"Are you a homosexual?" one fan magazine asked James Dean in the early 1950s, a question that is still debated. "No, I'm not a homosexual," the surly young star supposedly replied. "But why go through your life with one hand tied behind your back." There you have it. Although Dean may have been referring to the quip that bisexuality doubles your chances of scoring with someone (he was almost certainly bisexual), it also smacks of cold-blooded opportunism, which always has and still does define sexual activity in Hollywood. It's called the casting couch. Such a callous attitude about making it in Hollywood would have come naturally to Dean, who, throughout his short career, never hesitated to make the most of the manifold opportunities that were offered him. Dean lived for two months in 1951 (in Los Angeles) and six months in 1953 (in New York) with the openly gay radio and television director, Rogers Brackett, whom he met while working as a parking lot attendant at CBS and who was instrumental in getting Dean some early television jobs. Dean, who at one time was carrying on an affair with a male friend *and* his girlfriend, had a well-deserved reputation for callous promiscuity. And he did hang out at both the Friendship, a gay bar in Santa Monica, as well as at the Club, a leather bar in East LA, where he was said to have indulged a sado-masochistic penchant by having patrons put out cigarettes by grinding them into his naked chest. On September 29, 1955, the evening before he left on his fatal trip in the silver Porsche that subsequently unleashed an emotional necrophilia unmatched even by the death of Valentino in 1926, Dean attended a gay party in Malibu, which supposedly ended with a screaming fight with an ex-lover who accused him of dating women just for the publicity.

Calculated or not, Dean's performance with the women he dated must have been convincing. Although the luminously beautiful actress Pier Angeli married singer Vic Damone soon after Dean's death, she never got over her love for him, committing suicide in 1971 after writing a friend that, for her, "love died in a Porsche."

According to the then powerful gossip columnist Hedda Hopper, when she asked Dean how he avoided being drafted into the army when America was deeply involved in the Korean War, he said that he told the Selective Service he was gay. "I kissed the medic," Hopper quotes him as saying.

In the late 1940s, Rita Hayworth was Hollywood's reigning sex goddess and Columbia Pictures's most valuable property. Nevertheless, she and Harry Cohn, the studio's powerful founder, fought constantly over her private life and money.

Hollywood's Favorite Son of a Bitch—Columbia's Harry Cohn

Will we ever forget how Robert Duvall, Marlon Brando's consigliere in Francis Ford Coppola's *The Godfather*, convinces a Hollywood studio mogul that he'd better cast an over-the-hill pop singer named Johnny Fontane in a sure-to-be-hit movie that would revive his career? Early one morning the producer awakes to find the severed head of his prize racehorse lying next to him on a blood-soaked bed. He's convinced.

Welcome to Hollywood storytelling, where, since the very beginning of the film industry, fiction has endlessly been pollinated with fact. From Vito Corleone's olive oil business in *Part I* to the shenanigans over Vatican finances in *Part III*, much of the *Godfather* series' story line was based on Mafia legend. But a lot of it—certainly the casting of the fictional Johnny Fontane in a movie that would rebuild his career—was also based on Hollywood gossip. Everyone knew that Fontane's character was meant to represent Frank Sinatra. Though Sinatra was once the idol of millions of bobby-soxers, by 1952 his career was in a downspin; he'd lost much of his voice, one biographer speculates, because of nervous tension, and he flopped in a television variety series. As with Fontane, apparently thanks to Mafia pressure, Sinatra was cast in a film that would put him back on top. It was Columbia's 1953 war epic *From Here to Eternity,* and Sinatra's portrayal of Maggio won him a Best Supporting Actor Oscar.

But in this case, the director, as well as Mario Puzo, the author of the novel on which the movie was based, may have been far more accurate in milking Hollywood legend than most realized.

You won't find it mentioned in any biography of Harry Cohn, the boss of Columbia Pictures, the studio that made *From Here to Eternity,* but the horse's head scenario from *The Godfather* was probably an accurate retelling of the way Cohn may have been forced into casting Sinatra in the film. Most biographies of the studio chief attribute the selection of the pop singer to the friendship between Ava Gardner (Sinatra's wife at the time) and the studio chief, and the unavailability of Ernie Kovacs, the actor both Cohn and the film's director, Fred Zinneman, wanted in the role (Kovacs was committed to star on Broadway in Tennessee Williams's *Camino Real*). But Ann Miller, who made a dozen films for Columbia in the 1940s and knew Cohn well, claims that everyone in Hollywood suspected at the time that the real reason Sinatra got the part was that the Mafia—or someone interested in seeing Sinatra get the role—sent the studio boss the severed head of one of his favorite ponies. The rest was casting history.

If true, it was one of the few times in his career that Harry Cohn, a man who became probably the most hated studio boss in Hollywood because of his arrogance and vindictiveness during a thirty-seven-year career, was ever thwarted. Much has been lost in

Hollywood since the so-called golden age ended sometime in the 1950s, when the old studio system was beset with both the loss of their monopoly of the industry and the failure to understand and cope with the challenge of television. But perhaps the greatest loss was the very philosophy behind the making of films. Critics continue to bemoan the quality of films cranked out in Tinseltown these days; a seemingly endless parade of ever more expensive and ever more hollow blockbusters that, more often than not, capture and hold audiences not with the quality of the storytelling but with the quantity of special effects. As the cost of making and marketing movies escalates in some cases well past the hundred-million-dollar mark, the green-lighting of film projects has less to do with art than with the bottom line. Hollywood has been taken over by committees of bean counters.

Profit has always been the primary aim of filmmaking, but a half century ago there was always the chance you could make a film just because you wanted to make it—and damn the profit considerations. One example, *Citizen Kane*, is probably the best film ever made in America; for decades it was a money-loser. Even Joseph Kennedy, a man who was obsessed with making a profit on anything he did, be it rum-running, owning a studio, or cornering a stock, realized that moviemaking could never be solely dictated by the bottom line. He once warned against too much business pressure in moviemaking, saying: "Movie production requires producers . . . men with a flair for showmanship and an instinct for dramaturgy, men who could orchestrate the sound and fury of which pictures are made."

In his time, there was no producer more powerful than Columbia's Harry Cohn, a man filled to the brim with sound and fury who, unlike rival studio chiefs Louis B. Mayer and Jack Warner, held the dual reins of both studio president and production boss.

Because of his legendary abuse of his stars, writers, directors, and other producers, in his time he was often called the most hated man in Hollywood. "I don't get ulcers," he once said. "I give them."

Gossip columnist Hedda Hopper called Cohn "a sadistic son of a bitch," and the *Saturday Review*, then an important media opinion maker, called Cohn "an arrogant, uncouth, lecherous and relatively benevolent despot." Frank Sinatra, understandably, had nothing but nice things to say for the man who provided the vehicle for his career comeback. "A friend, a real friend" was Old Blue Eyes' opinion.

Despite roles in Capra's (and Columbia's) *Mr. Deeds Goes to Town* and *You Can't Take It with You*, Jean Arthur fought constantly with Cohn over her assignments to other film dogs and filled ten years of her career with invectives and lawsuits to gain freedom from her contract. When she finally won her independence in 1944, she ran through the streets of the Columbia lot shouting, "I'm free! I'm free!" (Irene Dunne and Cary Grant were two other actors who also publicly fought with Cohn).

Often Cohn's rudeness was calculated but by the 1950s his reputation had become so poisonous that few imagined someone so boorish could be that calculating. A perfect example is his treatment of Judy Holliday, star of the hit Broadway comedy *Born Yesterday*, for which Cohn spent a million dollars, the most money ever paid for screen rights up to then, despite the fact that the character of the junk dealer, Harry Brock, was modeled on Cohn. The comedy's writer, Garson Kanin, even told him so. The problem was that Holliday had trouble controlling her weight; in fact, Cohn often referred to her as "that fat Jewish broad." But after seeing her in the Katharine Hepburn/Spencer Tracy comedy *Adam's Rib*, Cohn agreed to cast her in *Born Yesterday*.

Holliday's weight remained a problem; Cohn knew it, but he

also knew her potential. After a late-night arrival in Los Angeles, she was immediately driven to the studio and ushered into Cohn's imperial office. The story goes that Halliday walked up to the desk and reached to shake his hand. Cohn ignored her greeting, got up, walked around her, and said, "Well, I've worked with fat asses before." A completely intimidated Holliday lost fifteen pounds before actual filming began, and the rest is film history. *Born Yesterday* became Columbia's biggest comedy hit since the glory days of the 1930s, and Judy Holliday won an Oscar for her performance, beating out Bette Davis for *All About Eve* and Gloria Swanson's now iconic star turn in *Sunset Boulevard*.

It is sometimes hard to separate the myths from the facts about Hollywood's stars and star makers as it is about the movies they made. But we do know that despite his frequently brutal methods Harry Cohn (helped immeasurably by the movies of Frank Capra) did make Columbia Pictures one of the film capital's top five studios, along with MGM, Paramount, Warner Brothers, and Universal, during the years he led it. Part of the reason was undoubtedly his swashbuckling, megalomaniac personality. In his time, Cohn's behavior was accepted as part of the personality of a pioneer; exploiting and humiliating talent as if he owned them was little different from the way Louis B. Mayer or Jack Warner treated their talent—Harry Cohn was just more public about it.

Unlike Mayer, who had as a talented production director for the decade of the 1930s the resident genius Irving Thalberg, Cohn was the be-all and end-all of his studio, the life and soul of Columbia Pictures. His involvement included judging whether a film would hold an audience's interest in an unusual way: "My ass itches if it goes on too long," he said. And, if there is one common denominator among the films he made or distributed, from the early one-reelers of the teens through the Capra films of the 1930s and his great films of the 1950s (among them Elia Kazan's *On the Waterfront* and Otto Preminger's *Anatomy of a Murder*), the best Columbia pictures didn't dawdle. Lacking MGM's vast capital reserves, Columbia simply couldn't afford to fail, and if Harry Cohn's itching ass was a barometer of success or failure, it proved to be at least as good a divining method as many employed by the industry before and since. Cohn clearly understood the impact of his personality and obviously didn't object when it was used to inspire vivid portrayals of the megalomaniac tycoon, including Broderick Crawford's Oscar-winning performance in Columbia's *All the King's Men* (1949) and the fictional portrayal of Harry Brock in *Born Yesterday*. It is also said that the character played by Everett Sloane in 1948's *The Lady from Shanghai* was modeled on Cohn by the film's director, Orson Welles, then husband of Columbia's biggest star, Rita Hayworth, and that Cohn was the model for the tycoon in Clifford Odets's 1948 play, *The Big Knife*, as well.

Cohn's office, like that of many studio heads, was a pure reflection of his personality and was deliberately based on the office in Rome's Palazzo Venezia of Benito Mussolini, the Fascist dictator of Italy. It all started when a worker in Columbia's New York office put together a short documentary on Mussolini from outtakes of a filmed speech and newsreel coverage of his accomplishments. Narrated by newsman Lowell Thomas, the film, called *Mussolini Speaks,* cost only ten thousand dollars grossed an astonishing million dollars and earned Cohn an invitation to visit Rome and receive a decoration from the dictator. Although friendly biographers have said that the apolitical Cohn (he was a Republican only because other studio chiefs were registered Republicans) didn't understand Fascist politics, he certainly understood the Fascist style. On his return he remodeled his office suite at the studio to resemble Mussolini's both in length and through installation of a platform on which his huge desk was placed.

The whole arrangement started with an outer office where a secretary would screen visitors and buzz them into an inner office and waiting room staffed by Cohn's personal secretary and a couple of assistants. It was here that the famous Cohn "treatment" began, as visitors, whether they had an appointment or not, would be subjected to a wait the length of which was previously determined by Cohn. It might be several hours for someone temporarily out of favor with the boss, or even several days as might be the case with an agent who either Cohn didn't like or who might be representing an actor in disfavor. The entrance to the inner sanctum was a huge, padded door that, having no handle on the outside, could only be opened by a buzzer at Cohn's or his secretary's desk.

On entering the inner sanctum, one walked through a long, carpeted room toward Cohn, seated at his huge, elevated semicircular desk, placed in front a display of what would eventually number fifty-two Oscars won by his studio. When invited, visitors would seat themselves on a sofa, only to discover that the springs had been weakened to lower them even more below Cohn's imperious gaze. On the desk were numerous telephones and an interoffice switchboard, allowing the mogul to demand that his operators find anyone in the world anytime or order his employees to his office with the invariable command: "Get your ass down here." On the wall opposite the window overlooking the Gower entrance to the studio (which enabled Cohn to check the on-time arrivals of his employees) there hung, at least until World War II, an autographed picture of Mussolini. Another door led to Cohn's private bathroom, which doubled as a barbershop and dental clinic. (Cohn, after learning that Mussolini considered the pain of dentistry without anesthesia a form of self-discipline, emulated the practice.) From his office another door led to his private projection room and to a passage that provided a separate entrance when he didn't want anyone to know he was there. It also led to the female stars' dressing room, where he, like many studio chiefs before and since, sexually indulged his power to make a female star rich and famous. In his storeroom, fine French perfumes and fur coats were stocked as gifts for reward and seduction—no cigarettes, though, in this era when smoking was prevalent. Smoking was banned on the lot.

Harry Cohn moved as swiftly as any of Columbia's films. Born in New York City on July 23, 1891, Harry was the third of five children (four boys and a girl) born to Joe and Bella Cohn, a German tailor and his Polish wife. Life was hard; years later Cohn would explain why he worked so relentlessly: "So *my* sons won't have to sleep with their grandmother."

Like his older brother Jack, Harry left school at fourteen to start working. He held jobs as a choir singer, as a shipping clerk in a music publishing business, as a trolley car conductor, and most successfully as a song plugger, selling song scores by singing them for theater and nickelodeon audiences. He also picked up extra money by hustling bowlers at nearby alleys. Cohn was always sensitive about his lack of a formal education, and it occasionally betrayed him; once, during a pep talk with his staff in the 1930s, he spelled out the name of his studio cheerleader-fashion, C-O-L-O-M-B-I-A, and was rebuked publicly by writer Norman Krasna; years later he made the same mistake when again challenged to spell the name of his studio.

For a while, he and a fellow member of the Wendover Avenue Gang named Harry Rubenstein teamed up as a song-and-piano vaudeville team. Years later, Rubenstein, then known as Harry Ruby and a successful composer of Broadway musicals, moved to

Hollywood and, with a partner, wrote songs for all the studios. All except Columbia; from early experience he knew Cohn too well for that.

Jack was by then working in New York for Carl Laemmle, whose Universal Pictures was cranking out one-reelers for nickelodeons (there were more than five-hundred in New York City) as fast as they could make them. Then, in 1913, he gambled on a much longer film, a sleazy exploitation film about the white slave trade called *Traffic in Souls*; the film cost $5700 but, thanks in part to Harry's salesmanship, grossed nearly $500,000 and established two rules followed by the film industry thereafter: the public likes feature-length movies and, even more important, sex sells.

With his brother and fellow Laemmle employee Joe Brandt, Harry formed his own production company in 1920 and set up shop on Hollywood's Poverty Row, a strip of storefront studios on Sunset Boulevard between Gower and Beachwood. The trio dubbed their new production company CBC, but because it was quickly dismissed by competitors as "Corned Beef and Cabbage," he patriotically renamed the operation Columbia four years later. Like all the Poverty Row studios, survival was a day-to-day business and financial solvency was dependent on making films as cheaply as possible. One of Harry's innovations was painting flats on both sides so that the same set could be used for different scenes; he also employed actors on the way up or down instead of contract stars ("The Port of Missing Stars" was a description of Columbia by one critic of the era). Like many early filmmakers, Cohn kited checks between coasts; California bills would be paid with checks on New York banks and vice versa, thus picking up some four to five days extra time to make the checks good while they were being transferred across the country.

In 1926, determined to escape the stigma of Poverty Row, Columbia bought a lot around the corner on Gower complete with a couple of open stages and a rickety office building (expanded throughout the years, Columbia would remain there until the early 1970s). The first film from the new studio was a financial gamble that increased the friction between Harry and Jack, whose conservative ideas about spending money would always be a thorn in Harry's side. Harry won his bet and, at the same time, convinced the fledgling industry that he was a serious player by booking the premiere of the movie, a big, expensive adventure film called *The Blood Ship*, at the Roxy in Manhattan, the country's biggest and most prestigious movie palace. Cohn, incidentally, would remain a gambler all his life. During the 1940s he would risk up to $15,000 a day on horse races. After being admonished by his board for losing $500,000 in one season, he switched to betting on football games.

The Blood Ship was a silent film made in 1927, the same year that Warner Brothers, only a few blocks down Sunset Boulevard from Columbia's new Gower Street studios, made what is generally (but not altogether accurately) considered the first talkie, *The Jazz Singer*. Making the switch to sound was a tremendous challenge for all of the studios, but Columbia had an advantage. As one of the only studios not to own a chain of exhibition houses, they didn't have to convert hundreds of theaters to the new technology as well as tackle the filmmaking process itself. This leanness also served Columbia well several years later when the Depression emptied many movie houses and bankrupted such large exhibition chain owners as Paramount and RKO.

Columbia began hitting the pace that was to make it famous in the 1930s, and Frank Capra basically made it happen. For years, because of its location on Poverty Row and because its main product was B movies and short subjects, Columbia wasn't taken seriously as a studio by most of Hollywood. Then, in 1927, a thirty-year-old immigrant Sicilian filmmaker with a gift for comedy named Frank Capra was hired away from Mack Sennett by Columbia to make a picture for a fee of one thousand dollars. The film, *That Certain Thing*, earned Capra a fifteen-hundred-dollar bonus and the enduring respect of Harry Cohn, and it launched a series of Capra films that brought the studio unparalleled fame and, not so incidentally, riches.

But as important as Capra was to Columbia, he wasn't the only director that added laurels to Harry Cohn's crown. Howard Hawks made *Twentieth Century* (1934) and *His Girl Friday* there; the latter, his witty takeoff on Ben Hecht and Charles MacArthur's play *The Front Page*, starred Cary Grant and Rosalind Russell in a film that set the probably still unbroken record for the fastest and some of the smartest dialogue in Hollywood history. It is as fresh today as it was when it was filmed over sixty years ago. Many of Cohn's best films from the next decade starred Rita Hayworth, an actress he claimed to have discovered, although she had previously made several films for Fox before being fired as unpromising. After a slow start at Columbia in such B films as *Girls Can Play* and *Paid to Dance*, Hayworth became an "overnight" star by stunning audiences with her beauty when she played Richard Barthelmess's wife in Hawks's *Only Angels Have Wings* (1939).

According to Ann Miller, who starred in Capra's *You Can't Take It with You* for Columbia two years before Hayworth's breakout performance in *Only Angels Have Wings*, Cohn liked Hayworth but was distressed over her choices for male companionship (for all his philandering, Cohn had a moralistically conservative streak). Cohn did, in fact, cough up the $30,000 demanded by Hayworth's first husband, Edward Judson, for a divorce at about the time Hayworth, on loan to Fox for *My Gal Sal*, became romantically involved with her costar Victor Mature. Judson, who had married Hayworth in 1937 when she was eighteen and he was forty, had given up a career selling automobiles to market his wife, which by 1942 was hardly necessary any longer. Hayworth starred in such film triumphs for the studio as 1944's *Cover Girl* and 1946's *Gilda*, in which Hayworth's striptease to the song "Put the Blame on Mame" helped make that film the actress's greatest hit, cementing her image as one of the all-time immortal sex goddesses of film.

During his Poverty Row days, Harry Cohn carried a torch for an actress he met in New York while still a song plugger. Her name was Rose Barker, but his move to California—not to mention her marriage to a rich lawyer—got in the way. Finally, after he was more or less established on Poverty Row, Harry invited Rose to visit. After her husband discovered what was going on, they divorced, and she married Harry the day the decree became final in 1923 (her $250,000 divorce settlement came in very handy for Cohn's business). The marriage, seemingly a good relationship in the beginning, began to deteriorate by the mid-1930s because of the time Cohn spent running his growing studio, his philandering, and, more important, Rose's inability to produce a child. Enter Joan Perry.

In 1935, Cohn met a young fashion model named Betty Miller at the Central Park Casino while on one of his contentious visits with his brother who ran Columbia's east coast operation (the problem, as it was for Louis Mayer, was that the New York office of several studios were the bean counters of the era; the people who controlled the money that the West Coast needed to make films). He offered her a job in films and changed her name (Betty Miller was too common in those days; "Perry" was the surname of a silent film star who had once captivated Cohn, and "Joan" was suggested by an assistant). Although she never starred in anything other than B movies, Perry soon became the star of Harry Cohn's life, despite his edict forbidding dating between Columbia's stars and employees, but the couple couldn't formalize the relationship until Cohn's private detectives caught Rose cheating on him, providing grounds for a divorce (they would remain friends for the rest of his life, however). Joan and Harry were married in New York on July 28, 1941.

Joan quickly became pregnant, but the baby girl died soon after birth (she was named Jobella, a combination of his parents' names that was also the name of Cohn's yacht). In April a healthy son whom they named John Perry Cohn was born; another son, Harrison Perry Cohn (who later changed his name to Harry Cohn Jr.) followed two years later.

Although the 1950s brought new riches to Columbia via such hits as *From Here to Eternity,* the biggest moneymaker in the studio's history, it also brought challenges. Among them was finding a new sex goddess to replace Rita Hayworth, who had left the studio when she married Prince Aly Kahn and—after returning and making such films as *An Affair in Trinidad* and *Salome* (1953), both of which failed to rekindle the male audience's libido—fought constantly with Cohn, primarily over money. And Fox had finally awakened to the dazzling sexual draw of a star who had previously made several unremarkable films for the studio. By 1952, when Twentieth Century Fox's *Niagara* was released, the studio began promoting her in a manner that can only be called salacious. Her name was Marilyn Monroe.

"We will make a star," Harry Cohn was reputed to have said when Hayworth walked out on what would be the last script offered. His choice in retrospect was odd: a twentyish Hollywood hopeful who—although she had appeared along with a lot of female extras in Howard Hughes's musical *The French Line*—like Judy Holliday was also inclined to fat and, unlike Holliday, couldn't act. At least that was the opinion of Cohn based on a screen test made during her tour as Miss Deepfreeze for Thor appliances. Her name was Marilyn Novak.

Despite his misgivings, Cohn bowed to his staff's recommendations and signed Novak to a contract; at $125 weekly, it was one of the cheapest in Hollywood. He also saw to it that her name was changed from Marilyn to avoid the obvious comparisons with Fox's star, and he demanded she wear a brassiere after the remake done by Columbia's costume designer, Jean-Louis, made it appear that she had no bust. Remembering his troubles with Hayworth, he demanded Novak not date anyone during the week and stationed a studio guard outside YWCA's Hollywood Studio Club, an all-girl residence where he required she live. Before closing in 1975, the Hollywood Studio Club, founded by Mrs. Cecil B. DeMille, housed some ten thousand young hopefuls over the years, including Ayn Rand, Linda Darnell, Donna Reed, and Marilyn Monroe in a spectacular block-long Mediterranean-style building designed in 1925 by architect Julia Morgan, who, five years earlier, designed San Simeon's famous main house and some of the guest houses for William Randolph Hearst. Located at 1215 Lodi Place, the Hollywood Studio Club, still owned by the YWCA, is now used as a Department of Labor career reeducation facility.

Despite Cohn's disdain for the renamed Kim Novak (he was soon referring to her as "that fat Polack"), she was cast in the fairly successful *Pushover* (opposite Fred MacMurray), *Phfft* (with Jack Lemmon and, wouldn't you know it, Judy Holliday), and, in 1954, *Picnic*, a challenging film that caused Novak, terrified over her own acting limitations, to suffer the first of a series of insecurity retreats. The frequent refusals to leave her dressing room so irritated Tyrone Power, star of her next film, *The Eddy Duchin Story,* that he commented to an interviewer: "[Her] confusion between temperament and bad manners is unfortunate."

For her next film, Novak was loaned out to star opposite Frank Sinatra in *The Man with the Golden Arm,* directed by Otto Preminger. Columbia was paid a hundred thousand for her time, she got $750 a week. This financial disparity came to a head with 1957's *Jeanne Eagels;* when she discovered that her costar, Jeff Chandler, was collecting $200,000 against her $13,000, Novak decided to hold out and Cohn placed her on suspension. His comments to reporter Ezra Goodman say much about Hollywood at the time and, in a way, explain why his management technique could be so brutal. "She's the number-one woman in Hollywood," he said of Novak. "Audrey Hepburn is the only one else. We've got twelve to fifteen million dollars invested in her. Stars believe [their] publicity after a while. I have never met a grateful performer in the picture business. . . . Hayworth might be worth ten or twelve million dollars today easily. She owned twenty-five percent of all the profits . . . and had hit after hit and she had to get married and had to get out of the business and took a suspension because she fell in love again! Think of what she could have made!"

1957's *Bell, Book, and Candle* with Jimmy Stewart, and Hitchcock's *Vertigo,* also with Stewart and made the following year, were probably Novak's best films—or at least the most representative of what was never more than a slight talent. But it was not Novak's acting that made headlines for her that year.

Late in 1957, Cohn discovered that Sammy Davis Jr. had asked Jerry Lewis to cover a Las Vegas gig so that the black entertainer could visit Novak in Chicago, her hometown. In fact, Davis went to Chicago to propose to the woman who was now Cohn's top star.

Cohn was furious, certain that if the story of the explosive relationship got out, it would ruin Novak's career, in which he had invested so many millions of dollars. Her agent immediately told her she would be finished in Hollywood if she didn't end the affair, and supposedly, Davis's pal and former Novak costar Frank Sinatra also told Davis to "cool it" with Kim. Then, when she didn't back down, Cohn, according to one story, hired some thugs to take Sammy out into the Nevada desert and threaten him. Another, far more likely story, which ominously echoed the way Cohn himself had been pressured to cast Frank Sinatra in *From Here to Eternity* six years earlier, claimed that Cohn called friends in Chicago whose consigliere made Davis an offer he couldn't refuse: either stop seeing Kim Novak or no nightclub in America would hire him again.

Whatever the truth, a week later Sammy suddenly married a black chorus girl named Loray White in Las Vegas. Many people, of course, thought the quick marriage was cooked up by the fearful studio even though Davis always maintained it was legitimate. The couple separated only seven weeks later, and Novak has always maintained that she and Davis were only "good friends" with a "warm friendship." In any event, although it is certainly true that the public's views on interracial dating and marriage were far different in 1957 than today, the stigma of racism has ever since tarnished Cohn's image.

By 1958, Cohn's health was failing. Four years earlier he had had a growth removed from his thyroid gland, which, although it wasn't publicly acknowledged at the time, was cancerous. And by the time of his confrontation with Novak, he had a serious heart ailment that was beginning to sap much of the tremendous energy that had always been another hallmark of his personality. He could barely walk up stairs he had previously bounded up two or three steps at a time.

Cohn knew his days were numbered. Before leaving for his annual vacation at the Biltmore Hotel in Phoenix on February 22, he bought a plot for himself and Joan near the small, central lake in Hollywood Memorial Cemetery. When he interrupted his vacation and returned to Los Angeles for the funeral of his friend, MGM executive L. K. Sidney, Cohn told Sidney's director son George (*The Eddy Duchin Story, Jeanne Eagels, Pal Joey*), a man who was probably Cohn's closest friend and confidante, "Get me a box."

After the funeral, the couple flew back to Phoenix (Howard Hughes, then owner of TWA, had ordered the plane held for them while they attended the funeral). There, following a reception for distinguished guests of the Biltmore, Cohn became seriously ill and was rushed to the hospital the following day, February 27, 1958. He died in the ambulance.

According to biographer Bob Thomas, when his first son was born, Harry Cohn was so overcome with happiness that he told an assistant: "You know something? I'm so goddam grateful for being a father that I'm not going to be a son of a bitch anymore." It was only a few days before he crossed paths with the same assistant, and remembering his earlier vow, the man who was creating many of Hollywood's most imperishable film treasures said, "I can't stand the strain anymore. I gotta go back to being a son of a bitch."

It is said that, fearing that no one would show up for his funeral, the studio ordered all its employees to attend. Red Skelton, observing the resulting, huge crowd at the now renamed Hollywood Forever Cemetery is said to have quipped, "See, give the people what they want and they'll come out for it."

It could have served as Harry Cohn's motto.

The film that made Rudolph Valentino famous was 1921's *The Four Horsemen of the Apocalypse*, in which he played an Argentinian gaucho caught up in the chaos of World War I. The movie cost an astronomical (at the time) $640,000 but made an equally astronomical $4 million. Part of it was filmed at the San Fernando Mission, founded in 1797 by the Franciscans, where this rare picture of Valentino, relaxing between takes, was made.

The Great Ranchos, and What Became of Them

For generations until California became part of the United States in 1850, the Los Angeles basin—like most of the state—was ruled from afar by Spain and later, Mexico. For the most part, those faraway governments couldn't care less about what seemed to be mostly useless desert.

Although the first Indians probably arrived in Southern California some eight thousand years ago, it took a long time for anyone to pay much attention. Hernando Cortez, the Spanish conqueror of Mexico, named the future state when—thinking that the peninsula of Lower California where he landed in May 1535 was an island—he christened it with the name given to a fictitious, idyllic island kingdom of Amazons portrayed in a popular novel of the time. Still, despite the first exploration of the Los Angeles coast by Juan Rodriguez Cabrillo (whose name is still memorialized in many local street and building names), no one paid much attention for another two hundred and twenty-seven years.

Then, on July 16, 1769, the Franciscans headed by Fr. Junipero Serra and the Spanish military captained by Gaspar de Portola founded California's first mission in San Diego. Forty-three years later, Fr. Serra's work was completed with the establishment of his last mission just north of San Francisco, each a day's journey along what was called El Camino Real ("The Royal Highway"). That royal road linked towns like Los Angeles, Santa Barbara, and Monterey into a geographic entity and also connected huge ranchos along the route. But don't think for a minute that those ranchos or missions, granted by the Spanish Crown or, after 1822, the Republic of Mexico, were anything like the Ponderosa or *Dallas*'s Southfork. The closest comparison would be a feudal community of the Middle Ages, with their residents yoked by kinship or servitude to the don or the head priest, and occupied with converting Indians to Christ or raising herds of long-horned steers. They essentially provided the only substantial industry in Southern California for generations (seventy-eight thousand cattle roamed the LA basin in the 1860s)—supplying a hide and tallow trade with the United States.

Los Angeles was founded in 1781 as an agricultural center, but for at least another century the area was defined by the Mexican and Spanish land grant Ranchos. As late as 1850, when California was taken into the Union, fewer than 8,500 people—half of them illiterate Indians—lived in the county. By the mid-1850s the Ranchos began falling into American hands, some of them by accident when many non-English-speaking grant holders, not understanding the U.S. Congress's 1851 demand that all such land grants be reconfirmed, lost titles to their property. Then, after living for a decade or two like the dons they succeeded, the new owners began to subdivide and develop their land holdings into towns.

More than 150 real estate salesmen recruited by the Nebraska-born Harry Culver (a friend of I. N. Van Nuys, developer of much of the Rancho San Fernando, which gave its name to Los Angeles's gigantic northern valley) started selling plots in 1913 on what had been the Rancho La Ballona near present-day Los Angeles International Airport. Two years later, pioneer filmmaker Thomas Ince established his Inceville studios in what was already known as Culver City; in 1924 the forerunner of the studio that would one day become the world's most famous, MGM, was established nearby.

A surprising number of their names are still with us, memorialized everywhere, from the names of towns (the Rancho San Pedro became the harbor city of San Pedro) to those of streets: Santa Monica grew on parts of both the Malibu Rancho, granted in 1805 to Jose Bartolome Tapia, and the San Vicente y Santa Monica Rancho, which was granted in 1828 to Francesco Sepulveda, for whom a boulevard—one of the longest in the Los Angeles area—was named. La Cienega Boulevard also commemorates yet another, the Rancho Las Cienegas ("The Cottonwoods"), which in the 1920s was developed into what became much of the city's west central area.

Rancho Los Palos Verdes eventually became the peninsula of the same name and the harbor city of Wilmington, Rancho Los Alamitos, and Los Cerritos became Long Beach, while Rancho San Jose became Pomona. Glendale was developed on some of the thirty six thousand acres granted in 1784 to Jose Maria Verdugo, a corporal who retired there a decade later to raise cattle

Portola and Serra first arrived in the Los Angeles area on August 2, 1769, and camped on the banks of the Porciuncula River (really more of a creek), giving the site the name El Pueblo de Nuestra Señora la Reina de Los Angeles de Porciuncula (the town of Our Lady the Queen of the Angels of Porciuncula), which, before it became popularly known as Los Angeles, was referred to as El

Pueblo. The next day the group followed a trail the local Gabrileno Indians used to gather fuel from open pools of tar located several miles to the west, arriving at a "grove of very large sycamores," springs, and a stream of water "as deep as an ox." (Later settlers used the tar to roof their adobe houses, and the original Indian path eventually became the footprint of Wilshire Boulevard). The rancho that named for those waters that later occupied the site (Rodeo de las Aguas) was bought in 1854 for four thousand dollars in cash and notes by Benjamin "Don Benito" Wilson (a developer of Pasadena, Riverside, Alhambra, and Westwood, mayor of Los Angeles, and the man for whom the nearby Mount Wilson was named), and a Major Henry Hancock; together they farmed two thousand acres of wheat until a devastating drought wiped out farming.

In 1907, at the site of a tiny station known as Morocco Junction on the railroad line between Los Angeles and Santa Monica, an oil man named Burton Green headed the development through his Rodeo Land and Water Company of a city boasting broad, tree-lined streets and telephone connections with Los Angeles. Green named it after Beverly Farms in Massachusetts, where he had vacationed, and added "Hills," for the local landscape. That year the first house was built on a Sunset Boulevard lot (cost: one thousand dollars); five years later, the developer took what was then an enormous chance to attract interest in the new community by building a luxury hotel in the middle of a lima bean field.

The gamble paid off: The Beverly Hills Hotel was an instant hit and is today one of the most prestigious in the world. Rodeo Drive, now lined with representatives of some of the most famous retailers in the world (among them Cartier, Tiffany, and Hermes) recalls part of the name of the original rancho.

Hired to run the new hotel (she eventually bought it) was a

woman named Margaret Anderson who had previously run the fledgling Hotel Hollywood, built in 1903 in a new community a couple miles east. Like Beverly Hills, Hollywood was built on the grounds of a rancho, or, to be more accurate, parts of two of them; one named La Brea, the Spanish term for the tar seeping out of the ground near that Indian trail, the other, Rancho Los Feliz, originally granted to Jose Vincente Feliz when he retired as the Spanish Crown's administrator of Los Angeles in the late 1790s.

Some have written that many early filmmakers were little more than a bunch of bandits—cultural bandits, at minimum—out to make a fast buck. That was true in many cases; some of them, including Cecil B. DeMille, certainly could be categorized as bandits, in the legal sense anyway, having fled three thousand miles west to escape the patent laws owned by the Motion Picture Patents Company (generally called "the Trust") covering motion picture equipment. They also now resided close enough to Mexico so that they could cross the border if things got too hot. DeMille was certain there had been several attempts on his life by the Trust, and he slept with—and wore—a pistol for years.

Yet the behavior of some of the early developers of the original ranchos was as bad or worse. Take, for example, the man who made the huge, world-famous preserve on the north border of Hollywood, known today as Griffith Park, possible. He was a thoroughly unlikable person named Col. Griffith J. Griffith, not the director D. W. Griffith, as many think today.

After acquiring much of the old Rancho Los Feliz in 1882, Griffith donated 3,015 of the Rancho's 7,000 acres to the city for a park fourteen years later in gratitude for his prosperity (the balance of his acreage to the west and south was developed for residential use); it would be the largest park in any city in America. Although the Los Angeles city fathers accepted his gift two years later, they didn't want anything more to do with him. For one thing, the story got around that the only reason he gave away the land was to avoid paying taxes on it; for another, and far more damaging, it wasn't much later (1903) that Griffith, who made millions from mining investments, was convicted of shooting his wife. He also accused her, a devoted Catholic, of conspiring with the Pope to steal his money.

Once released after serving two years in jail for the attempted murder, Griffith started lobbying the city to accept the gift of an observatory for the park, which many considered nothing more than a crude ploy to buy back respectability. Even after he published a plea in 1910 that the city go ahead and develop the land he gave them for the public's use, nothing happened until he died nine years later. Only then did the city feel free to accept the $750,000 he willed it, and eventually it used the money to build the still popular Greek Amphitheater (1930) and the Griffith Park Observatory (1935).

Remember Henry Hancock? The money problems that forced him to sell his half of the soon-to-be Beverly Hills would have been history had he lived just a bit longer. Soon after Henry and his brother, John, acquired the Rancho La Brea, they began developing it commercially; the first investment was a refinery that produced five tons of asphalt daily from the fossil-filled tar pit for seventeen years until it closed in 1887. (Henry and Ida lived in a small frame house they built in a eucalyptus grove near the tar pits, the site of today's Los Angeles County Art Museum; today's West Hollywood largely sits on John Hancock's portion of the rancho).

In 1885, Henry's widow, Ida, began leasing out the oil exploration rights on most of the rancho; although the first well was dry, by 1910 the lessees' 250 wells were producing nearly 4 million barrels a day, and a corporate giant that eventually became the

Union Oil Company of California was launched. Ida received royalties of one-eighth of everything that came out of the ground, making her, at the time of her death in 1913, one of the richest women in the world. But she and Union Oil didn't get it all. Before the turn of the century, a man named Arthur Gilmore bought a small plot of land from the Hancocks near today's intersection of Fairfax and Wilshire Boulevard, to start a dairy farm. In 1903, while he was drilling for more water for his cows, Gilmore struck oil, and within months his farm was filled with derricks producing thousands of barrels of oil daily for what would become the largest independent oil company on the West Coast.

Gilmore's dairy farm is today the site of the world-famous Farmer's Market, founded in 1934, the same year that his son, Earl, built the eighteen-thousand-seat Gilmore Stadium nearby, which housed all kinds of open-air sports events for a generation, including football and car racing. A couple of years later Earl built the adjoining Gilmore Field, for years the home of the Hollywood Stars baseball team of the old Pacific Coast League, whose celebrity owners included Bing Crosby, Gary Cooper, Cecil B. DeMille, Walt Disney, George Burns, and Gracie Allen. The arrival of the Brooklyn Dodgers in Los Angeles spelled the end of the Hollywood Stars; their final game was played on September 7, 1957. The site of Gilmore's stadium and field is now occupied by CBS Television City. Recently, the Farmer's Market itself was expanded with a gigantic, singularly ugly mall addition, completely overpowering the rural charm of the original.

Such is progress.

Among the most famous talent agents was Paul Kohner, who represented dozens of major stars including Lana Turner, Robert Taylor,
Henry Fonda, Myrna Loy, and Peter O'Toole. Here he appears in the
late 1920s with Mary Philbin, who came to Hollywood after winning
a Chicago Elks Club–sponsored beauty contest at the age of seventeen. Philbin went on to make a number of silent films, most notably
1925's *The Phantom of the Opera*, for which she dubbed in her voice

The Ten-Percenter

Today, to be in Hollywood without a talent agent is to be nowhere. Actors, writers, directors, still or motion picture photographers—even trained chimpanzees—everyone and everything who wants to be in show business or appear to be in show business, needs a talent agent to get a job. And, most actors and filmmakers also need a publicity agent, who will labor to tell the world that you got the job your talent agent lined up for you or make sure the people who are doing the hiring know you're alive. And to pay the bills, of course you need a business manager.

And so it has been largely since the early days of film—at least since the days when actors ceased being anonymous and began to be "celebrities." A new, hybrid category has evolved to take over the responsibilities of talent and business management, simply called a "manager," since the big, factorylike agencies swallowed up the small, usually one-man (or woman) agencies beginning in the 1950s, when TV began scaring the hell out of everyone in Hollywood. By being big, these agencies also had the ability to put together an acting, directing, and production "package" taken from the roster of talent represented under one roof.

Today the cost of such a team can be high. A talent agent is allowed by law to no more than 15 percent of his or her client's income, but the manager can charge whatever the client will pay (usually 20 percent). Publicity agents usually charge a flat fee that can average another 5 percent. So figure a minimum of 25 percent for your team plus taxes, and that fabulous house in Holmby Hills with the Ferrari in its garage may be even farther out of reach than you think.

"Working your way up from the mail room" to become an agent or manager has become a Hollywood cliché. But, like most clichés, it has its roots in fact. In Hollywood it's always been "who you know" and there is no faster way of learning who the players are than in the mailroom of a major talent or PR agency. There is no better example than that of David Geffen, who started his career in the mail room at the New York office of the William Morris Agency before he became a music mogul. Today a billionaire, Geffen is a partner with producer/director Steven Spielberg and Jeffrey Katzenberg in the Dreamworks SKG film and television production entity.

There are a lot of famous agencies in Hollywood, among them Creative Artists Agency and Creative Management Agency, but, as important as they are, their operations can resemble, like film production itself today, that of a factory more than the hands-on, person-to-person relationship that was once the norm in Hollywood. Not that that was altogether better, but many of the old-time agents were well-mannered businessmen who did their jobs professionally and were generally liked by everyone. Then, as now, casting directors rely heavily on a few agencies—usually those with a stable of the most popular stars of course—so just getting an agent isn't the answer; if you're serious about working in the industry, you've got to get an agent who the casting people call, which is a challenge on an entirely different level. And, in any business, there are those who are more or less hated by everyone except, of course, the clients for whom they deliver the goods. Certainly among the latter was the rapacious Henry Willson, who is remembered today for creating the careers of (and new names for) Troy Donahue, Rock Hudson, and Tab Hunter.

There are few better examples of an agent who became famous representing many of Hollywood's greatest, from the sultry Pola Negri to the aristocratic David Niven, than a nice guy who started his career as a filmmaker for Universal Pictures' cofounder Carl Laemmle in the 1920s: Paul Kohner.

In the beginning, Kohner's road to success was navigated in much the same way as that of many film pioneers—by filling a vacuum created by the rapidly growing industry. In his case, it was by exploiting his German-speaking roots. First, Kohner, the eighteen-year old son of the owner of Teplitz, Bohemia's (now Czechoslovakia) only movie house, wangled an interview with Laemmle when the film mogul was taking the waters at the then-famous spa. Following the interview (and a no-holds-barred pinochle game), the president of Universal was so impressed with the young man's drive that he offered to bring him to America to learn business management. Within days of his arrival, Kohner, simply because he spoke German, was given the job of directing "foreign publicity."

He soon promoted a trip for himself back to Europe, arranging the premiere of Erich von Stroheim's film *Foolish Wives* in Monte

Carlo, where the film is set. It seemed like a great publicity ploy, but the principality didn't agree, since the film broke the absolute rule of never depicting the interior of the famed Monte Carlo casino, even if it was only approximated by a movie set. But Kohner did manage to wangle a medal for Laemmle from the president of Czechoslovakia based on his promise that Universal was planning to build a studio in the country. In short order he was on his way back to Hollywood as his boss's personal publicist and, in 1924, in one of the first such surveys, drove more than a hundred thousand miles across America canvassing exhibitors to learn what audiences really wanted to see.

Kohner also based his first movie, *Love Me and the World Is Mine,* on a popular Austrian novel, *Hanna and Her Lovers.* The screenings were disastrous, but Kohner, back in Europe, realized—with the same sense of human nature that one day would make him one of Hollywood's most successful professional matchmakers—what was missing. To bring his silent, slow-paced film alive for an important screening in Karlsbad, Austria, before an audience that would include Laemmle and Sol Lesser, head of the powerful RKO theater chain, it needed a musical score to be played by an orchestra in the pit of the theater. So he hired the local thirty-two-member civic orchestra to provide atmosphere by playing familiar Austrian tunes, including several Strauss waltzes and marches, as the film unreeled.

Witnesses say there wasn't a dry eye in the house when the movie played to its happy denouement; in any event, Lesser booked it and Kohner was on his way as a producer.

Although he was to make several more films, it was as Universal's newly appointed supervisor of foreign productions that Kohner came up with an idea that other studios swiftly copied. Before sound arrived, films could be shown anywhere with more or less the same success, and the overseas market was an important part of the financial success of a movie. But how could that profitable market be protected after the arrival of talkies in 1928, when all the characters were speaking English instead of miming their roles? His answer wasn't so simple, but it worked: start making the same picture in different languages. The first film made in a foreign version was ideal for such experimentation, as it was basically a filmed concert by Paul Whiteman's band called *The King of Jazz*. All Kohner had to do was line up a different master of ceremonies proficient in each of the foreign languages chosen: German, French, Spanish, Italian, and Japanese. The whole process was inexpensive, took only a few days to shoot, and the finished films looked like each had been especially made for their audience. It became far more complicated with nonmusical features since few actors—other than stars such as Dietrich, who could redo her films in German—were proficient in foreign tongues; nevertheless, until dubbing became commonplace years later, that's the way it was done. For his breakthrough, Kohner was rewarded with a twenty-five-dollar raise. It was a clear message that his future lay outside Laemmle's studio.

After several years of producing films and establishing a Universal studio in Germany, Paul found himself out of work when Laemmle sold Universal to a syndicate. An offer to join MGM evaporated with the sudden death of Irving Thalberg, the studio's young chief of production. With nothing else to do, Kohner rented an office, bought some furniture, ordered a telephone, and set himself up as an agent. He was now a seller in an industry where he had once been an all-powerful buyer of talent, a "flesh peddler," as they were then called, and worse, one without any clients.

That changed quickly when Kohner learned that Joe Pasternak, a producer at Paul's old studio, was looking for a script for his latest "discovery," a sixteen-year-old Canadian named Deanna Durbin. While visiting Universal, Kohner also ran into a screenwriter friend who was grinding out hack scripts for a puny salary, discovered he had a perfect property for Durbin, became his agent, and walked back across the studio and sold it to Pasternak for the then tremendous sum of thirty thousand dollars. It was the best money the studio ever spent. The story made the front page of both *The Hollywood Reporter* and *Variety*. The film was the 1936 musical comedy *Three Smart Girls*, and it not only made Durbin an overnight child star, but was largely instrumental in saving the studio from bankruptcy.

Reportedly, none of the million-dollar deals that Kohner was to later negotiate for clients, including Myrna Loy; Rita Hayworth; Lana Turner; Robert Taylor; David Nevin; Max von Sydow; Henry Fonda; the great character actor Walter Huston and his director son, John Huston; Charles Bronson and his wife, Jill Ireland; Mia Farrow; Liv Ullmann; Peter O'Toole; Mick Jagger; and Martin Sheen satisfied him as much as he regretted *not* being able to sign a deal for Greta Garbo with RKO at the end of her career. The film, *Iceland*, was written for Garbo by her friend Salka Viertel when the actress attempted the last of several comeback attempts in the 1950s. The problem? Garbo wanted to stop work at five every day; the studio demanded she work until six.

It isn't enough for most actors to have a talent agent; they also need a press agent. There is probably no profession in or out of Hollywood whose job description and performance standards are so vague. Supposedly a "flack's" job is to make a client, be it a film star, a movie, or, for that matter, a sanitation company, famous. There are even clients who pay high fees just to have their names kept *out* of the news. But the bottom line is that no one since the so-called public relations industry's beginnings in New York a century ago can promise to deliver *anything*. The public often confuses publicity with advertising. Advertising is when you buy space to say nice things about yourself, and publicity is when the media says something—preferably nice—about you. Accordingly, editorial space—that obtained through publicity or public relations—is always valued many times over advertising space. And many people—sometimes the practitioners themselves—are confused about the difference between publicity and public relations. It's also simple. Publicity is what you get by beating the drum for the client—think of a political campaign. Public relations is how you spin that publicity or dress a situation that is making its own news. Like a Pentagon briefing in wartime.

Unlike a talent agent, whose performance can be accurately gauged by the amount of work a client gets, what a publicist produces can often be nothing more than the luck of the draw. The problem is that the public relations professional can only supply media with ideas and news that they hope will result in "ink" or airtime for a client. Naturally, clients with a high profile such as Julia Roberts or Tom Cruise can get the press to roll over just about any time they want, but what about the actor who would like to become a Julia Roberts or Tom Cruise? It's a perfect Catch-22 situation—the press couldn't care less.

The days are long gone when you had three or four newspapers in the major cities, dozens of competing columnists, and three competitive news services. So there is simply not as much territory available to get a few breaks for the client. Thus, today, as a publicist, you either have to find clients who are happy to pay just to have their hands held, or have clients whom everyone wants to write about or talk to, or use your head and actually compete for coverage in an increasingly shrinking market.

One of the ways you can compete is to use a trick that publicists also have exploited from the beginning: make news. Now, for an individual star this isn't so easy; after all, not every hopeful female star, for example, would be willing to make news by riding a horse stark naked down Hollywood Boulevard (although some have tried); unless you're bucking for the role of Lady Godiva, there's not much of a future in that. But there are stunts that have resulted in a lot of media attention, such as walking between buildings on a tightrope or demonstrating fencing skills on television when the nearest the client has ever been to an épée was on the set of his latest film. It *can* work.

For films, stunt promotion can be really effective, if, on occasion, somewhat weird, like the time Cecil B. DeMille invited the press corps to watch—and meditate on—the filming of the crucifixion of Christ on Christmas Eve, 1926, during the production of *King of Kings*. A good Episcopalian like DeMille surely knew Christmas was a highly inappropriate date to promote Christ's *death* as a media event, and that reporters rarely meditate about anything.

It also helps when the publicity is linked to reality. One of the most effective campaigns, and one that galvanized a nation's anticipation of 1939's *Gone with the Wind,* was the endless tease over the search for an actress to play Scarlett O'Hara. Many stars, including Tallulah Bankhead and Paulette Goddard, were in the running, but the problem was real . . . David Selznick and the original director, George Cukor, simply had no idea who would play the part even after principal photography had begun. Then, on the first night of location shooting, Selznick's brother, Myron, a popular talent agent who represented Laurence Olivier at the time, showed up on the set for the burning of Atlanta (filmed with three different stand-ins for Scarlett) with Olivier's lover and future wife, Vivian Leigh, and the rest was Hollywood history. The timing and the strategy, we now know, was carefully worked out between Olivier, Leigh, and Myron Selznick, but that is exactly why it worked.

With the arrival of sound in 1928, the twenty-three-year-old multimillionaire Howard Hughes decided to remake his first film, a World War I epic called *Hell's Angels*, as a talkie starring Jean Harlow and Ben Lyon. He filmed at the Jasper Studios on Las Palmas Boulevard in Hollywood. The studio, renamed the Hollywood Center Studio, is still in business.

Hollywood, California, Thursday, November 15, 1928

In 1920, F. Scott Fitzgerald introduced the flapper in his first novel *This Side of Paradise*. Modeled on his wife Zelda, she was the embodiment of youth, possessed a lithe, boyish figure, wore her hair as short as possible (usually in a new style called the bob), and was known for her impetuosity, whimsy, and boundless energy for having a good time. And, of course, the most crucial ingredient was youth itself.

So on a hypothetical day, say Thursday, November 15, 1928, let's follow the adventures of a fictional, twenty-one-year-old Hollywood flapper and movie hopeful named Darla Devereux. That's not her real name, of course; like most people determined to break into movies, our heroine followed the example of the successful actors and actresses and adopted a stage name . . . the more exotic, the better (like Pola Negri, who was really Apolonia Chalupec from Lipno, Poland, or Valentino's wife, Natacha Rambova, born Winifred Kimball Shaughnessy in Salt Lake City). Born Ruby Johansen in Rembrandt, Iowa (population three hundred), Darla, like thousands of others, was drawn to the film capital by dreams of film celebrity and riches. After working on the fringes of the film industry for months as an extra (and turning down countless propositions from men claiming to be casting directors who could give her a break for a few "favors"), today she finally has, as the then popular phrase went, a "leg up" on the competition. Thanks to her boyfriend—let's call him Mitch— who not long ago traded a career as a movie star hopeful for the fairly new profession of talent agent, she'll be auditioning for a part—albeit a small one.

Then, as now, it isn't what you know, it's who you know, and Mitch knew the comely assistant to the film's producer and director, a twenty-three-year-old multimillionaire named Howard Hughes, then struggling to make his first film, a silent war movie named *Hell's Angels* (which included buying and reconditioning nearly a hundred World War I fighters).

After rolling out of bed in the tiny bedroom of her tiny Gower Street clapboard courtyard apartment to the clang of her Little Ben alarm clock, Darla showered, toweled her fashionably short, bobbed hair dry, and donned her chenille bathrobe before retrieving a quart bottle of Adohr Farms milk (its cream on top clearly visible in this prehomogenized era) from her doorway stoop. After turning on her Zenith tube radio so that it could warm up, she put the milk in her tiny Norge refrigerator (which she and everyone else called an icebox) and set the coffee to percolate on the gas burner. Sponsored by Lucky Strike cigarettes, the news that day was mostly about Herbert Hoover, the new president-elect who had swamped the Democrat Al Smith in the election a couple weeks earlier, and his plans after he took office in March (Inauguration Day would be shifted to January 20 in 1937). There was also an interesting item about Anna Anderson Monahan, who had earlier announced that she was the Grand Duchess Anastasia Nikolayevna, the daughter of the late Russian Czar Nicholas II who was supposedly killed with the rest of the Romanovs eleven years earlier (not until DNA tests in 1993, nine years after Monahan's death, was her claim finally disproved). Then there was a short item about Eleanor Garatti, who won a gold and a silver medal in the Amsterdam Olympics earlier in 1928 (the first in which women participated), followed by the familiar news about the apparently unstoppable stock market boom. Less than a year later, of course, America would discover the boom wasn't so unstoppable on Black Tuesday, October 29, 1929. And, always part of local news coverage, there were the latest stories, speculations, and rumors about the movie industry.

It was going to be a full day, Darla realized as she sipped her coffee; after the audition she planned a trek downtown to shop for a birthday present for Mitch at the Broadway Department Store (the Hollywood Broadway branch was completed but not yet fully stocked), and she wanted to look her best. So there was no question about what she would wear: it would be her favorite, good-luck outfit—the dark-red wool skirt and jacket with a matching cloche hat that she bought with the twenty-five dollars sent by her parents as a early Christmas gift. Combined with a crisp, ecru silk blouse, she'd look as good as, so the popular phrase went, "the bees' knees."

First thing, though, would be brunch with her agent on the sprawling front porch of the Hollywood Hotel, which had overlooked Hollywood Boulevard from the days it was still an unpaved, dusty or muddy—depending on the weather—thoroughfare known as Prospect Boulevard. (The legendary hostelry, built in 1903, was torn down in 1956. On the site today is the new Hollywood/Highland complex with the Kodak Theater, which in March 2002, after three quarters of a century of Academy Awards ceremonies, became Oscar's first permanent home). As the weather was typically splendid for Los Angeles in November, Darla decided to walk to the hotel, passing along the way Columbia Pictures Studio at the corner of Gower and Sunset Boulevard (now the Sunset-Gower studios), the open-air market near Hollywood and Vine where she often bought the oranges she loved (then rarely found in winter back home in Rembrandt), the new Hotel Roosevelt and, across the street, Grauman's Chinese Theater. It was there that, a year and a half earlier and freshly arrived from Iowa, Darla joined a crowd of a hundred thousand to watch Doug Fairbanks and Mary Pickford, the king and queen of Hollywood, arrive for the theater's opening with the premiere of Cecil B. DeMille's *King of Kings*. "Someday they'll want the impression of my hands and feet in the cement in front of the theater," she dreamed as she passed the theater; the popular practice had been started soon after it opened.

After meeting Mitch, the pair ordered the popular dish invented in New York in the 1890s, Eggs Benedict. Few paid any attention to calories or cholesterol then . . . at the time, "California cuisine" implied the use of citrus in food rather than the lean cuisine the term would signify two generations later.

After brunch, it was only an eight-block walk to the Jasper Studios at 1040 Las Palmas Boulevard where *Hell's Angels* was being made. (From 1980 to 1983, the place housed Francis Ford Coppola's Zoetrope production company. It is now the Hollywood Center Studio.) Like everyone else, they swept past the "Public Not Admitted" at the gate and walked into the normal chaos of a movie lot where they immediately spotted Howard Hughes, fashionably if incongruously dressed for golfing in plus fours, plaid socks, and a brown V-neck sweater. He was sprawled in a canvas director's chair and surrounded by his crew outside one of the new sound stages. Introductions would have been quickly completed, and although Darla was prepared to make a screen test, this was not the day. All Hughes wanted to know was what she looked like and, as important, how her voice sounded.

"I think you'll do just fine," Hughes may have said to her in his Texas drawl. "Do you have a telephone?" (It would be a year before the first telephone was even installed on the president's desk; until then President Hoover used a phone in a booth outside his office.) "No? Well, stop by the studio and see my assistant in a couple days . . . you know her already. She'll set up a screen test." Needless to say, Darla was floating on air as she left the studio lot and walked back up to Hollywood Boulevard to catch the Red Car that ran directly downtown.

The Pacific Electric Railway and its Red Cars were only one part—albeit at 1105 miles the largest—of the huge urban transit system that crisscrossed the Los Angeles basin from the teens until the 1950s, when it was replaced by buses and the tracks largely torn up. In the 1920s and 1930s, one could travel from the ocean in Santa Monica to the desert climate of San Bernardino— seventy-five miles east—for pocket change, and the later loss of the Los Angeles basin's unique rail system to the freeways, many of which follow the old railroad rights-of-way (as do today's new urban railroads) was one of the great tragedies in twentieth-century urban planning.

Today, Darla's trip was fairly short (nine miles), but it was easily the most popular ride on the line, because just before ending its route in the subterranean bowels of the gigantic new Subway Terminal Building at 417 South Hill Street near downtown Los Angeles' Pershing Square, the cars of the two-year-old Hollywood extension roared through a mile-long tunnel under Bunker Hill, invariably thrilling all aboard.

The Red Car soon arrived (they ran at ten-minute intervals during the day) and Darla boarded, deposited her fare (a dime), and settled back on the rattan seat for the scenic ride downtown. One thing she immediately noticed as she looked back, after glancing at the HOLLYWOODLAND sign built atop nearby Mount Cahuenga four years earlier to advertise a real estate subdivision, were the electric Christmas trees being readied for the first Santa Claus Lane parade (they plugged into special outlets at the base of the streetlights). Mixed in the traffic there also seemed to be a vastly increased number of the Ford Model A automobiles that replaced the venerable Model T the year before. Accompanied by the metallic squeals of the trolley's wheels and the blare of its horn, her Red Car soon turned past Echo Park Lake, across which Darla could see Aimee Semple McPherson's Angelus Temple, which she once visited and where she saw the famous evangelist, accompanied by a squad of church members (many of them movie stars) dressed as football players, "score a touchdown for Jesus."

Before she knew it, the trolley was in the tunnel and she was downtown. Although it was a bit of a hike across the terminal's marble floor to reach the outdoors, the Broadway department store was right across the street. A music lover, Darla first checked to see what was new in that department. She wasn't disappointed; there, with the sheet music essential for making your own music, a still common practice, was the score for "Sonny Boy." It was the song that made *The Singing Fool*, the movie she and Mitch were going to see tonight, famous. On display also was the latest phonograph record by her favorite classical singer, Amelita Galli-Curci, then probably the most famous soprano in the world: "Home, Sweet Home" coupled with "The Last Rose of Summer." Darla wanted it for herself, to add to her small collection of records—mostly popular, sentimental favorites by Galli-Curci—played often on her windup Victrola, but the five-dollar cost of the Victor Red Seal 78 rpm disk was not in her budget today.

So Darla wandered into the book department, and there, displayed next to A. A. Milne's new *The House at Pooh Corner* and the popular *Oxford Book of Carols* was the perfect gift . . . or, more accurately, two perfect gifts for Mitch: the new edition of F. Scott Fitzgerald's 1924 novel *The Great Gatsby,* and the just published *All Quiet on the Western Front* by Erich Maria Remarque (it would be made into a movie starring Lew Ayres the following year and win two Oscars: Best Picture and, for Louis Milestone, Best Director). Frustrated by the choice, she bought both (for $1.95 each), went to the store's lunchroom, and ordered a toasted cheese sandwich and a Coke.

It was only about three o'clock when the Red Car deposited Darla back in Hollywood, so she decided to relax for a while in the ornate, Spanish Colonial lobby of the community's newest landmark, the towering Roosevelt Hotel, which had opened a year and a half earlier. Named for Teddy Roosevelt, the place had been built by a syndicate that included Mary Pickford, Douglas Fairbanks, and Louis B. Mayer.

During the years following Darla's visit the hotel would become a playground for Hollywood. In 1932, a penniless, twenty-two-year-old David Niven would live in a staff room he'd remember as being "no larger than a broom closet." A couple of years after that—about the time that Errol Flynn was mixing martinis in the hotel barbershop—Bill "Bojangles" Robinson would teach Shirley Temple a tap-dance number on the lobby's tile stairway. The would make it famous in 1935's *The Little Colonel*. Still later, a frequent visitor to the hotel's popular Cinegrill was Marilyn Monroe, who posed for her first ad—

for suntan lotion—on the diving board of the hotel's pool. But the reason that the Roosevelt Hotel will live in film history is because it was the site of the first Academy Awards ceremony.

On May 16, 1929, less than six months after Darla's visit, the first awards (presented for movies made in 1927 and 1928 and then called Merit Awards) were handed out by Academy of Motion Picture Arts and Sciences president Douglas Fairbanks and Cecil B. DeMille's brother, William, at a banquet for 250 people (who paid ten dollars apiece) in the Roosevelt's Blossom Room. The very first recipient was Janet Gaynor, who won the title of Best Actress for three films: *Seventh Heaven*, *Street Angel*, and *Sunrise*. Best Actor was Emil Jennings, for *The Way of All Flesh* and *The Last Command*. Best Director awards were given to Lewis Milestone for *Two Arabian Knights* (Comedic Picture), and Frank Borzage for *Seventh Heaven* (Dramatic Picture). The Best Picture was *Wings*. Two honorary awards were given: one to Charles Chaplin for versatility and genius in acting, writing, directing, and producing his movie *The Circus*; and the other to Warner Bros. for producing the movie that revolutionized the industry by introducing sound the previous year, *The Jazz Singer*. The ceremony, during which thirteen statuettes were given out, took only five minutes to complete.

The award that one day would symbolize the ceremony was a twelve-inch high, gold-plated statuette of a naked knight holding a sword and standing on a reel of film. Designed by MGM executive art director Cedric Gibbons, it was known for years simply as "the Statue." So, how did it end up being known as "Oscar"? Although some credit Bette Davis for naming it after her first husband, Harmon Oscar Nelson, Jr., most film historians trace it to an Academy librarian named Margaret Herrick, who said it reminded her of her uncle Oscar.

But Darla wouldn't have known any of this, of course; for her, it was just a pleasant hour spent watching the world go by. Soon she returned to her apartment, where she might have taken a nap before preparing for her evening with Mitch. Following another shower, she donned one of her most glamorous frocks, a dark-blue silk sheath topped off with the silver-fox fur-piece her mother had given her when she left Rembrandt. Mitch was taking her to the Musso & Frank Grill, one of Hollywood's most popular restaurants (it still is), followed by a screening of *The Singing Fool,* playing at the brand-new, sound equipped Warner Theater on the nearby corner of Hollywood Boulevard and Wilcox Avenue. The movie was Al Jolson's second feature, made right after the stunning success of *The Jazz Singer.* In it, he plays a successful singer who goes on the skids when his small son dies; more important, he sings the sentimental "Sonny Boy,"—the first million-selling popular song— and "Rainbow 'Round My Shoulder." It was the first blockbuster talkie and was said to have been the biggest grossing motion picture before *Gone with the Wind,* eleven years later.

Following a dinner of pre-Thanksgiving turkey and stuffing preceded by an order of broiled grapefruit (then faddishly popular) and ending with a chocolate sundae, the pair wandered over to the theater. Darla was thrilled to see that in addition to the movie, on the bill was *Steamboat Willie,* the animated cartoon about a character named Mickey Mouse by someone named Walt Disney that got a big reception at its premiere ten days earlier at New York's Colony Theater. Darla loved the movies, crying when Al Jolson's son dies and laughing over the antics of Mickey Mouse. But she was ready to go to bed when Mitch took her home.

Darla Devereux and Mitch are fictional, but everything she saw or experienced that day was real or it could have been . . . so much was happening in her adopted home of Hollywood, and so much would continue happening over the next years.

Not only was MGM's legendary designer Adrian responsible for creating Greta Garbo's "look," he also created the broad-shouldered, narrow-hipped style that is inseparable from our images of Joan Crawford. And, while he was at it, he also created the legendary ruby red slippers worn by Judy Garland in *The Wizard of Oz*.

Film's Fashions

For more than a generation between 1920 and the advent of television in the 1950s, nothing had a greater influence on what American women (and many men) wore or wanted to wear than the movies.

Movies were not only the cheapest form of entertainment but also the broadest-based means of communication, spreading—deliberately and sometimes subliminally—advanced ideas in social behavior, popular culture, and fashion. By the 1920s, the American woman was also exercising her emancipation from the strictures of the Victorian Age. It was only a generation earlier that most women were treated more as objects than as people—how a woman looked was immensely more important than what she thought. In fact, the curvilinear look of the turn-of-the-century's Art Nouveau design style was based on the corseted, wasp-waisted women's fashion then popular. And, of course, there were millions of men who sincerely believed that women couldn't think, anyway, at least not objectively enough to vote, a right denied "the fairer sex" by the founding fathers.

World War I, with its demand for an expanded workforce plus the social blurring wartime inevitably brings about, helped change matters and was capped by the ratification of the nineteenth Amendment to the Constitution in 1920. Finally, a half century after the vote was extended to former male slaves and seventy years after the birth of the women's suffrage movement, women could finally vote.

In the opening sequence of *Possessed,* a hit film of 1931 starring Joan Crawford and Clark Gable, there is a sequence that speaks volumes about the times, women's dreams about re-creating themselves, and how one went about accomplishing it. (The sequence is today far better remembered than the movie itself, through its inclusion in 1992's compilation film about American cinematography, *Visions of Light*).

Crawford's character, Marion, is seen standing at a railroad intersection after a day spent working at a paper-box factory. While she's standing there, a passenger train passes slowly, each window revealing an aspect of the good life Marion dreams of, with the final pair of windows revealing a couple dressed in evening wear, dancing and embracing.

The train then stops, and a passenger, carrying a glass of champagne, starts a conversation with Crawford/Marion. "You know," he says, "there's something wrong with you." Marion replies: "There's everything wrong with me—my clothes, my shoes, my hands, the way I talk. But at least I know it." Notice the order: fashion first, then manners, as it always has been since the days when dress was the primary way of identifying status and power.

Emboldened, Marion decides to do something to change her

luck. She moves to New York and reinvents herself by learning how to dress, order food in French, and play the piano. She also becomes the mistress of a wealthy man who, after the standard won-loss-won-again plotline, eventually marries her and thus legitimizes her transformation. At one point he asks her if she has any regrets. Crawford, speaking as much for herself and a generation of Jazz Age hedonistic hopefuls as for her own character, replies: "I never learned how to spell regret." The line was the sort that never would have been uttered by "America's sweetheart," Mary Pickford.

In her time, Pickford was the most famous actress in the world—probably the most famous *person* in the world. She started the first fashion craze in America—not for the costumes she wore in such movies as 1917's *Rebecca of Sunnybrook Farm* but for her famous, little-girl curls. Despite the continuing popularity of Pickford's look with the older generation, only a few years later, jazz babies were shingling off sweetheart curls as fast as they were shortening their skirts. At the same time, they were remaking their bodies with, seemingly, the speed of light, transforming the big-busted, hourglass shape favored by their mothers into a near breastless and hipless androgynous form. In less than a decade, film audiences also switched their allegiance from the sweet (Pickford was reaching the point where she had to move into mature roles, anyway) to the sexily tantalizing, making stars out of sultry talent as Greta Garbo, Marlene Dietrich, and Joan Crawford.

But that's not to say that all fashions changed at once. In retrospect, the 1930s may be seen as the heyday for such sirens as Garbo, Dietrich and later, Hayworth and Crawford, but the most popular box office stars of the era were another eternal, curly-haired child, Shirley Temple, and, of all people, Marie Dressler, a lovable character actress but, built as she was along the general lines of her transportation in *Tugboat Annie*, surely no candidate as a clotheshorse.

But the world was changing, and those changes opened the door to something that, other than being employed in some silent historical dramas as a visual calling card for depravity, had rarely been breathed in film: lesbianism. When Dietrich sailed to America and Paramount in 1930, her legs, thanks to her performance as the cabaret singer Lola-Lola in the same year's German-made film *The Blue Angel*, were sensationally famous. But before revealing those famous legs in her first Hollywood film, *Morocco,* she first appears in a top hat and tuxedo—nearly as startling to audiences as appearing naked would have been.

Although it was first a publicity stunt (there is a famous picture of Dietrich and the aviatrix Amelia Earhart both wearing mannish gear), Dietrich and many of her friends—the most famous of them Greta Garbo—were soon flaunting the style offscreen, too. The media was quick to notice, and much of it deplored the trend; in 1933, one New York tabloid claimed (on the basis of a poll supposedly taken at a local girl's school) that it reflected the desire of 40 percent of the women interviewed to be men (actually, when it came to equal opportunity in the workplace, that part of it probably was true). The tabloid went on to quote the prediction of a New York University professor of abnormal psychology that since "this is still a man's age, and our society is based on masculine values," the trend was nothing but a fad that would soon pass. So much for prophets; in hindsight, the popularization of trousers for women was, clearly, one of the most significant fashion trends of the twentieth century.

At first, audiences considered the style more amusing than anything; a "continental" rather than "American" look. But it wasn't long before such homegrown talent as Katharine Hepburn and

Carole Lombard as well as their female fans jumped on the bandwagon; one survey taken in the mid-1930s on the corner of Hollywood Boulevard and Vine revealed that out of forty-seven women interviewed, eighteen—nearly 40 percent—were wearing pants. Unsaid and largely unknown to the vast majority of moviegoers, and despite the adoption of the fashion by such heterosexual stars as Hepburn, wearing pants was a visual code between lesbians.

Not everyone was convinced of the trend toward more mannish fashions for women; Mae West, for one. Until exaggerations overtook her image, she was an icon of femininity to millions of fans. In fact, in a sort of mini-reaction to the masculine influence on women's fashions, her 1933 film *She Done Him Wrong,* in which West sashays around in Gay Nineties costumes, actually revived the hourglass shape in Paris where "Mae West Parties" became the rage. So popular was the fad that the Parisian couturier Elsa Schiaparelli based her entire collection the following year on the "Mae West Look," and, in fact, during the 1930s, hems descended again.

But enough women were convinced where the future of fashion would lead that a more masculine look in daytime, evening, and athletic designs began to reach Main Street. As many discovered, however, it took more than a well-upholstered pocketbook to join the trend. Broader shoulders and narrower hips in clothing demanded, as did many previous and subsequent fashion statements, that many women reshape their bodies, and a rage for slimming started. One cereal company advertised that its product helped women achieve the "gracefully rounded curves" (read "thinner") demanded by the new fashions. Also popular on women's college campuses in the late 1920s was something called the "Hollywood Eighteen-Day Diet" (reflecting the acceleration in all our lives since the golden age of film, a much-advertised weight-loss formula of today is the "Hollywood Forty-Eight-Hour Diet").

Nevertheless, such self-help formulas were seen as a weakness of the newly liberated female by Madame Silvia, the health guru *Photoplay* brought on board in January 1933; readers who had a problem losing weight, she asserted, were just "lazy."

Padding the shoulders of women's clothes made them seem broader and the wearer more "in charge." And, although the style was started (also by Schiaparelli) in the late 1920s, it was a Hollywood designer, hitherto best known for designing the costumes for two of Rudolph Valentino's last three films, who would popularize the look worldwide. Along the way, he would become the film capital's most famous and probably greatest designer, creating costumes for 233 films during a three-decade career (most of them for MGM, where he conceived the indelible style forever associated with Marlene Dietrich, Jean Harlow, and, most famously, Greta Garbo). In the course of designing the costumes for 1939's *The Wizard of Oz,* he also achieved film immortality when he had red sequins hand-sewn onto a piece of pink chiffon, which was in turn hand-sewn onto a pair of patent leather shoes, thus creating Judy Garland's ruby slippers. His name was Gilbert Adrian.

Born Adrian Adolph Greenberg in Naugatuck, Connecticut, March 3, 1903, Greenberg attended the New York School for Applied and Fine Arts and for two years designed costumes for Broadway shows such as Irving Berlin's high-styled *Music Box Revues,* housed in the still-standing Music Box Theater Berlin built at 239 West Forty-fifth Street.

In 1923 he moved to Hollywood and changed his name to Gilbert Adrian; for the rest of his life he would always be known simply, as his later MGM contracts stipulated, as "Adrian." There are rumors that the young designer—who was gay—had a teenage affair with Rudolph Valentino before the future Latin lover moved from New York to Hollywood in 1920, but they have never been confirmed; what is known is that soon after his arrival, Adrian was hired by Rudolph Valentino's wife, Natacha Rambova, to assist in designing costumes for the actor, receiving sole screen credit for the outfits for 1925's *Cobra* (costarring Nita Naldi) and *The Eagle*, a period-costume adventure set in Catherine the Great's Russia.

Period costumes defined much of Adrian's career and included Garbo's *Queen Christina* (in which the costumes were less remembered than Garbo's controversial, full mouth kiss of her lady in waiting, Elizabeth Young), *Anna Karenina* (1935), and the following year's *Camille*. But it was through designing a non-historical costume for a 1932 melodrama called *Letty Lynton* that Adrian first created what would be his signature look and, coincidently, transform the public image of the film's star, Joan Crawford, from that of a party girl to an internationally recognized clotheshorse and, according to media of the time, "the most copied girl in the world."

It was just one of the gowns in the film that did it. Listed as "dress number 578" and made in the MGM workshop where Adrian supervised, depending on a particular film's requirements, a small army of up to 250 cutters, tailors, beaders, embroiderers, jewel craftsmen, feather workers, and seamstresses, the costume was made of white and apricot-rose organdy. But it was its design, broadening Joan Crawford's shoulders with huge padded and ruffled shoulders and lengthening the torso to make her hips look smaller, that started a rage; reproduced by many, one version sold more than a half million copies at Macy's in only months.

Not only was the design popularized by the movie, it was also the way it was used in *Letty Lynton* that fueled romantic dreams of millions. Fleeing from a vicious lover in South America, Crawford/Letty, on board a ship to New York, seeks solace in the arms of Robert Montgomery. Most of Crawford's gowns—like those of many other successful actors—were designed for their ability to catch light and were crucial elements in defining character. But this one was special. In the film, the dress's moonlit waves of ruffled organdy frame and soften Crawford's face, giving her a look of innocence and vulnerability that is particularly attractive to Montgomery, elements that are also crucial in setting up audience sympathy for a character who, in a later attempt at suicide, will accidentally kill her former lover.

So successful was the design that Crawford wore similar gowns in later films; perhaps it was the way that it combined the contradictory fashion trends—the "feminine" puffed shoulders evocative of the Gay Nineties "mutton" sleeves matched with the "masculine" connotations conveyed by the narrow hips.

Four years before *Letty Lynton*, Adrian had already created a fashion rage that would last a decade with the slouch hat he designed for Garbo in *A Woman of Affairs* followed by her sultry outfits in 1931's *Mata Hari*. It was the beginning of a generation-long friendship so close that when Garbo unofficially left films following the disastrous reviews of 1942's *Two-Faced Woman*, Adrian retired from film as well. But long before that would come to pass, Adrian far surpassed his colleagues in Hollywood in the number of films he costumed.

In July 1928, two months after his twenty-fifth birthday, Adrian signed his first contract with the newly formed Metro Goldwyn Mayer for five hundred dollars a week. For thirteen subsequent years, he would dress many of the studio's self-proclaimed inventory of "more stars than there are in heaven"; his billing would be "Gowns by Adrian."

Like the *Letty Lynton* dress, the velvet ostrich-feathered hat partially covering one eye that he designed for Garbo to wear in

1930's *Romance* and the pillbox hat he created for her in 1932's *As You Desire Me* were also widely copied; so was the snood designed for Hedy Lamarr in *I Take This Woman* (1939). For Jean Harlow, Adrian produced many slinky, figure-hugging dresses; like many of his gowns, these were cut on the bias. Besides the bold silhouettes created by padded shoulders and longer waists, Adrian also liked asymmetric lines and diagonal fastenings. The use of fashion to gain a better life, first used by Adrian in Crawford's *Possessed,* was a technique later used by many directors (including Adrian) in many films. Among them is 1937's *The Bride Wore Red,* in which Crawford's lust for a form-fitting, bugle-beaded Adrian sheath in shaded tones of red (which made it even more figure revealing), seems greater than the lust she harbors for her two bland suitors, an aristocratic playboy (Robert Young) and an annoying philosophical postman (Franchot Tone).

Selling copies of fashions seen in films became so profitable that several franchise operations were set up to sell them in shops and department-store boutiques; the first was Waldman's Cinema Fashions, which launched its enterprise in 1935 with authorized knockoffs of the dresses worn by Ginger Rogers in *Flying Down to Rio,* a film whose central sequence is a fashion show hosted by Fred Astaire. Another was the Studio Styles line launched by Warner Brothers the same year.

Author Howard Gutner has called Adrian's creations "potent artifacts of the American dream—of that limited and romantic vision of life's possibilities that once dominated American film." Nevertheless, Adrian always turned down offers to mass-market his designs, claiming that "they will never faithfully reproduce your clothes." He chose, instead, to open his own couture in Beverly Hills in 1942 after quitting MGM and, aside for a dozen or so films over the next decade, leaving movies as well.

This was not the case with Adrian's Warner Brothers rival, who went by the stage name of Orry-Kelly and who would become famous for designing the costumes in such films as *The Maltese Falcon* (1941), *Casablanca* (1942), and 1958's *Auntie Mame*.

Born in Australia in 1897, Jack Kelly moved to New York in hopes of becoming an actor but, because of his talent for art, began his career painting nightclub murals and silent film titles during the early years of silent movies. Eventually he began designing theater costumes for the Shubert reviews, *George White's Scandals*, and other Broadway productions, especially those starring Ethel Barrymore. Then he and the twenty-eight-year-old Archie Leach moved to Hollywood in 1932 and both changed their names: Kelly became Orry-Kelly and Leach, of course, Cary Grant. During the course of his career, Orry-Kelly was costume director of Warner Brothers for eleven years (he was introduced to Jack Warner by Grant), and he also designed for Ingrid Bergman, Marilyn Monroe, Dolores Del Rio, Kay Francis, Ruth Chatterton, and, most famously, Bette Davis. Throughout a long, devoted friendship, Davis called him her "right hand" and relied upon his costumes to define her characters.

Adrian never won an Academy Award because the category wasn't added until after his retirement from film, but Orry-Kelly shared an Oscar with Walter Plunkett and Irene Sharaff for *An American in Paris* (1951) and won on his own for *Les Girls* (1957), *Some Like It Hot* (1959), and *Gypsy* (1962).

In 1939, Adrian married Janet Gaynor, an extremely popular star who had won the first Oscar for Best Female Actress in 1929 (awards in those early years were given for an actor's body of work the previous year). Janet Gaynor was one of the few actors to successfully make the transition from silent to sound films, receiving an Academy Award nomination for her most famous role starring with Frederick March in 1937's *A Star Is Born*.

Adrian died in Hollywood of a heart attack on September 13, 1959, some time after he returned from Mexico, where he had retired to paint. Gaynor died in 1982, two years after she was seriously injured in an auto accident in San Francisco with her longtime close friend Mary Martin.

Before his death in 1964, Orry-Kelly summed up his career with the somewhat cynical remark: "Hell must be filled with beautiful women and no mirrors."

And, although Adrian may have sounded nearly as cynical when he attributed his 1942 retirement to Greta Garbo ("when the glamour goes for Garbo it goes for me as well"), he also credited too much of his fame to Crawford ("Who would have thought," he once said, "that my entire reputation as a designer would rest on Joan Crawford's shoulders?"). But it was, in fact, Joan Crawford who probably paid the designer his most generous compliment. Recalling her Oscar-winning performance in 1945's *Mildred Pierce*, she said, "It was not one of the dozens of films that made the critics rave about the way I dressed. No Adrian. I looked crummy through the whole thing."

Today the films of Frank Capra may seem simplistic, but in the Depression and war-plagued 1930s and 1940s, their theme that suc cess came from self-reliance and by doing the right thing greatly appealed to most Americans. They also made Capra the most suc essful director in Hollywood. Here he directs Claudette Colbert and

John Doe Meets Hollywood

"Maybe there really wasn't an America,
maybe it was only Frank Capra."
                    —Actor John Cassavetes

A century and a half ago, among the most profound influences on American culture and thought was a series of over one hundred books written to inspire young people by teaching them that courage, faith, and hard, honest work was the path to overcome hardship and achieve success. Horatio Alger Jr.'s rags-to-riches novels, most featuring homeless newsboys and bootblacks from the streets of New York City who succeed through pluck, self-reliance and always doing the right thing, were an instant success and remained so for generations. Part of the reason was that they were easy reads, their moral lessons illustrated by example instead of by preaching. Another was that they caught and clarified the spirit of the country—or at least a simplistic utopian America to which our ancestors gave lip service.

In the 1930s and 1940s, similar impulses sped the astonishing rise—literally from rags to riches—of the director Frank Capra. His films, despite frequent sentimental and simplistic themes that once set sophisticates' teeth on edge, largely defined the home of the brave to itself and to the world. It could never happen again. For one thing, the Depression-era populace that was reassured by Capra's simplistic stories is long gone. And the social, economic, and, more important, professional environment of Hollywood in its golden age that allowed Capra's talent to blossom so brilliantly have been swept away by the bean counters, television's one-size-fits-all homogenization, and the mega-budget action films made possible by advancing technology and an ever younger audience. Nevertheless, to millions, Capra's themes still resonate so loudly that they have become part of today's film iconography; one only need consider the frequency of television reruns of such movies as *Mr. Smith Goes to Washington*, with its scathing—if simplistic—portrait of political corruption, and, especially, *It's a Wonderful Life*, today as inextricably linked with the holiday season as Santa Claus, more than two generations after it was made in 1947.

Capra himself compared his movies and his life to Horatio Alger's work; when he wrote of his progress from an impoverished, immigrant childhood in Los Angeles (he was even a newsboy) to film immortality honored by three Oscars: "Conquering adversities was so simple I began to think of myself as another Horatio Alger, the success kid, my own rags-to-riches hero."

But it was never as simple as he claimed in his 1971 autobiography, *Frank Capra, The Name Above the Title,* a story of success so streamlined that one critic called Capra "a legend in his own book." Since his death, there have been the expected revisionist biographies pointing out that some parts of his own memoirs were self-serving inventions, including even the title of the book itself, reflecting Capra's assertion that he was the first director to get his name on theater marquees. D.W. Griffith was actually the first with the release of *The Birth of a Nation* in 1915, but Capra does seem to have been the first director who didn't own his own studio to be so honored. Despite the award of the Congressional Medal of Honor, presented to Capra by President Franklin D. Roosevelt for his wartime *Why We Fight* film series, there are those who believe he hated Roosevelt for his social and big-government policies. Years later, Capra was obviously feeling much the same way when he told an interviewer that he resented African-Americans because they "expected compensatory special treatment rather than lifting themselves up by their own bootstraps," as he believed he had done. And biographer Joseph McBride (*Frank Capra: The Catastrophe of Success,* 1992) asserts that with his last film, 1961's *A Pocketful of Miracles* starring Bette Davis, Capra pitted the movie against the "hedonists, homosexuals, hemophilic bleeding hearts, the God haters who cried, 'Emancipate our films from morality.'" In any event, that movie pointed up a sad decline in his box office clout; to make the film, he was forced to take on the popular actor Glenn Ford as coproducer. "What choice would I make . . . principle or money?" Capra said later. "I opted for money. And Frank Capra became a paper tiger."

A Pocketful of Miracles, a clumsy, static remake of his 1933 *Lady for a Day,* was a failure and deserved to be one; watching it today can be an excruciating experience. In an apparent effort to retrieve public respect, Capra defensively blamed the failure not on the reactionary themes he espoused in the movie but on the one thing his characters could never be accused of, a lack of principle on his part. "I sold out the artistic integrity that had been my trademark for forty years," he said in his autobiography. "[My] 'thing' with the people lost its magic, and the people said, 'Capra—we've had it with you!'"

Revisionist critics have also categorized much in his films as "embarrassing" and "pure corn." Embarrassing? Depends on your point of view and where you draw the line between sentiment and sentimentally. Corn? Absolutely—and Capra knew it, occasionally describing his sentimental storylines as "Capra-corn."And, as far as portraying himself as a Capra-esque hero in *The Name Above the Title*? One doesn't need to be a psychiatrist to see his background and self-image at play. Recalling the teenage Capra, the historian of his 1914 Manual Arts High School graduating class said in 1980: "I don't know that anybody really liked him. He was ostracized; people never invited him anywhere. Because he was a foreigner, they didn't think of including him in their parties. He was a nice boy. He was just a terrible wop." In 1932, when Lucille Reyburn, his soon-to-be second wife, asked him about their prospects for marriage, the Roman Catholic Capra reminded her that her father believed "all Catholics and foreigners have leprosy." Many celebrities, far less socially handicapped than Capra felt himself to be, have dosed up far more fiction in telling their stories.

Some thirty years ago my mother and I visited the director and his wife (who was always called "Lu") at the Wells Fargo Bank in Indian Wells, California, which then doubled as a Catholic church on Sundays (despite her parents' problem with the union, the couple remained happily married for their lifetimes). In his seventies and retired from Hollywood to the desert where he had so many times retreated in earlier years to work out thorny script and production problems, the deeply tanned director was ebullient and full of anecdotes. "How's retirement?" I asked at the close of our visit. Capra grinned from ear to ear, threw a stage wink, and shot back what was by then a well-practiced rejoinder: "Great!" he said. "It's a wonderful life!" Then he laughed heartily.

Frank Capra seemed clearly to be a happy man. Why not? As *Time* said in a 1938 cover story when Capra was forty-one, his life was better than his film stories.

The future film director was born on May 18, 1897, in the tiny village of Bisaquino, Sicily, the sixth of seven children born to Salvatore and Rosaria Capra. (He later changed his middle name from Rosario to Russell because he felt that made him sound less like a "dago immigrant").

According to his memoirs, Frank Capra's youthful hegira to filmland's mecca began with a letter to his forty-seven-year-old father from a friend of his long lost older brother, Ben. According to Capra, since no one in his family could read, the local parish priest read it to them (another piece of petty fiction from Capra; it's true about the priest reading the letter, but his mother was literate). As the letter explained, Ben, who had disappeared from the face of the earth—Sicily, anyway—five years earlier, had run the thirty miles to Palermo, where he shipped out on a Greek freighter. After more than two years wandering the globe, he had ended up in Los Angeles and now invited the family to join him.

As Capra remembered it, the journey undertaken by his parents and the four youngest children (the two oldest girls were married and remained in Bisquino) seemed like twenty-three days in purgatory; thirteen of them storm-tossed in the filthy, overcrowded steerage hold of the steamship *Germania* (during which Frank celebrated his sixth birthday), two in the overcrowded pandemonium of Ellis Island, and eight more on equally overcrowded trains headed west with only bread and fruit to eat. When the little family finally arrived, Ben met them at the city's Southern Pacific station, took them to a nearby church to thank God for their safe passage, then brought them to a house he had rented for them on Castelar Street (near today's Little Tokyo section in downtown Los Angeles).

The Capras were fairly lucky. Within a month everyone had jobs: Rosaria in an olive factory; Salvatore as a sort of human conveyor belt in a glass bottle factory, carrying thousands of glowing, red-hot future olive bottles six at a time from the furnaces, and the kids in candy and soda shops. Of the children, only Frank attended school, contributing every cent he made selling newspapers with his brother Tony to the family's funds (when trade was slow, Tony punched Frank to attract attention and make his papers sell quicker). Capra's embarrassment over his roots never faded. Explaining why he went to the newly opened Manual High School in 1909 (where he worked as a part-time school janitor) instead of the more upscale Los Angeles High, he wrote: "[I] belonged to the riff-raff of Dagos, Shines, Cholos, and Japs." Clearly the reason had more to do with geography than racial profiling and he went anyway, determined that although "born a peasant . . . I'd be damned if I was going to die one."

After graduating at sixteen, Frank worked six months as a pipe welder's assistant and saved seven hundred dollars to study engineering at the school that would be renamed the California Institute of Technology in 1920. He commuted on a used motorcycle between the school, a twenty-five-cents-an-hour janitorial job at the Pasadena Light and Power Company, and the lemon grove fifteen miles away where his father had resettled the family. He graduated in June 1918 and joined the U.S. Army because "all Bluebloods enlisted; Noblisse Oblige stuff." After an armistice-foreshortened military career, Frank returned to Los Angeles, bade farewell to his mother (Salvatore had died in an accident harvesting lemons, and Rosario had moved the remains of the family to another house near downtown Los Angeles) and set out to make his fortune.

Like many ambitious young men, it took Frank Capra a while to figure out just how he was going to make that fortune—three years, in fact, during which he hustled poker games, picked oranges at twenty cents a day, played guitar in bars, tutored the son of Lucky Baldwin (discoverer of the fabulously rich Nevada silver mine known as the Comstock Lode), and sold worthless mining stock door-to-door. Capra rarely admitted ever selling such "blue sky" stock as it was derisively called; some cynics, however, credit the experience with giving the future film director an unerring sense of the public's gullibility, which the future director deliberately exploited in later years.

Capra declined the offer of a job in San Francisco to use his chemical engineering skills to design stills for a syndicate of Sicilian bootleggers before fate struck in the form of an advertisement for a job at a local film studio. There, he directed his first film for a retired Shakespearean actor named Walter Montague; it was a one-reeler based on a poem by Rudyard Kipling titled *Fultah Fisher's Boarding House*. In 1924, he married a part-time actress named Helen Howell, joined the Hal Roach Studio in Los Angeles as a writer for the *Our Gang* series, and later left to work as a gag writer for Hollywood's "king of comedy," Mack Sennett. While there, Capra claims, it was through his direction that a previously unsuccessful comic named Harry Langdon was turned into a star overnight via such hits as 1926's *Tramp, Tramp, Tramp* (which Capra also wrote), *The Strong Man* (1926), and *Long Pants* (1927). When Langdon moved to First National Pictures, Capra went with him but was soon fired by the comic, who, like many stars, made the mistake of believing his own publicity (Langdon's fame fizzled as fast as it ignited; he died, forgotten, in 1944).

Capra's marriage collapsed quickly. Howell was from a rich family that impressed the twenty-seven-year-old Capra: "I loved her for that. I liked classy gals," he said. But, based on the experience of two previous failed marriages, Howell wasn't happy with his all-consuming passion for work. Capra admits he was "married to movies" and that the "studio was his home." He was also embarrassed that his wife got along well with his family. In a section of his autobiography that he later cut, Capra wrote contemptuously of her rapport with his mother and siblings and the lifestyle they represented. The marriage ended in 1927.

After a stint in New York, where Capra directed 1927's *For the Love of Mike*, his first flop and today remembered largely because it was the first film of a young, Parisian-born comedienne named Claudette Colbert, Capra returned to his new home on Odin Street near the Hollywood Bowl and went back to work writing gags for Sennett. Three months later, Columbia Pictures, then still a ramshackle studio on the section of Sunset Boulevard known as Poverty Row, telephoned. (A popular nickname for the studio was "the germ of the ocean," a parody of the opening "gem of the ocean" lyrics of the then popular patriotic tune "Columbia.") Harry Cohn, the irascible head of Columbia and a man with the reputation for chewing up artists like a barracuda, wanted the out-of-work Frank Capra to direct a movie. After a contentious meeting, the always-adversarial Cohn reluctantly agreed to pay Capra, who had been paid six hundred dollars weekly (six thousand in today's money) for his previous film, a flat fee of a thousand to direct. It was the beginning of a thirteen-year relationship with Cohn, during which Capra would make twenty-five films—all but two among his best—win all three of his Oscars, and see his income soar to three hundred thousand per picture. Those films were also responsible for catapulting the underdog Columbia onto the short-list of Hollywood's major studios and making Frank Capra the most talked about director in town.

It didn't happen overnight. Capra's first film for Columbia was a quickie, seven-reel comedy called *That Certain Thing* made for half of what Sennett paid for a two-reeler. It made money and Cohn increased his fee to twenty-five hundred for each of the two following films, a pair of comedies called *So This Is Love* and *Matinee Idol*. Again, Cohn liked what he saw on the screen and in the box office, offered Capra a one-year contract at five hundred weekly, and loaned him seventy-five hundred dollars to buy a Malibu beach house complete with a tennis court that the director had once rented for a vacation and loved.

Capra was also learning one of the essentials of early filmmaking: improvisation. In 1929's *Submarine*, he filmed an underwater rescue scene using a two-foot submarine bought for fifty cents and a tiny toy metal diver bought in a nickel "claw" machine in his corner drugstore. He made *Rain or Shine* (1930), far funnier than the Broadway musical on which it was based, by throwing out the music. In the following year's *Dirigible*, set in frigid Antarctica but filmed in the summertime heat of Los Angeles, Capra wanted the actors' breath to show, so he improvised small metal cages to put in their mouths to hold dry ice; it worked perfectly, except for one actor who lost part of his jaw and several teeth by refusing to use the cage.

He was every bit as imaginative when it come to casting. In 1930, Capra gave Barbara Stanwyck her start in the otherwise forgettable *Ladies of Leisure*, followed by *Miracle Woman*, in which the actress played a cynical, Elmer Gantry–style revivalist in a satire inspired by Hollywood evangelist Aimee Semple McPherson. This was followed by *Forbidden,* a film Capra categorizes as "99.44% soap opera . . . saved from the 'loss' column . . . by the performances of Barbara Stanwyck, Adolphe Menjou, and Ralph Bellamy." 1933 saw Stanwyck's breakthrough film, *The Bitter Tea of General Yen*, memorable not only for her sensual portrayal of an

American missionary who has a love affair with a Chinese warlord but also as the film that opened New York's prestigious Radio City Music Hall. It was also one of Capra's few money-losers, primarily because it was banned throughout the British Empire because of its interracial love affair.

Then, after 1934's *Lady for a Day* (based on a Damon Runyon story Columbia bought for fifteen hundred dollars and the director's first big hit), Capra made film history with a movie that, despite a lukewarm reception when it opened (also at Radio City Music Hall, where "the critics," Capra says, "were caught with their adjectives down"), became one of the most popular of film classics. Made in four weeks for $325,000, it was the film industry's first masterpiece of screwball comedy, and still reigns as the first of only three movies ever to sweep Oscar's five major categories: best film, best actor (Clark Gable), best actress (Claudette Colbert), best director (Capra), and best screenplay (by Capra's friend and associate Robert Riskin)—*It Happened One Night*. It would be forty-one years before this record was equalled by 1975's *One Flew Over the Cuckoo's Nest* and then sixteen years more before *The Silence of the Lambs* matched the record in 1991.

According to Capra, *It* also happened by accident. While he was in Palm Springs writing *Lady for a Day*, Capra went to have a haircut and, while waiting for a barber, picked up a copy of *Cosmopolitan* magazine. In it he discovered, read, and was captivated by a short story by Samuel Hopkins Adams called "Night Bus," a comic romance set in real locations such as buses, diners, and that newest of American travel phenomena, motels. After a battle, Capra convinced the reluctant Cohn, who believed that audiences didn't want trivia like "bus" pictures, to buy the property for five thousand dollars. He set about casting the movie and soon discovered that actors didn't think much of his "bus" picture either. Myrna Loy was the first to turn down the lead, believing that although the comedy routines were good, the characters—a rich spoiled heiress and, in the first script, a vagabond painter (later a crusading reporter)—were unsympathetic; then Margaret Sullavan and Miriam Hopkins turned down the picture ("Not if I *never* play another part," Hopkins snapped) and, finally, Constance Bennett offered to buy the script and have it rewritten for her. Seeking a light comedian for the male lead, Capra asked MGM to borrow Robert Montgomery, but he turned it down, too.

Then Capra got a break. Louis B. Mayer wanted to discipline an MGM actor who was demanding more money by temporarily exiling him to a studio in Poverty Row. His name was Clark Gable, and Capra had his understandably reluctant (at least initially) male lead. To play the heiress, Capra finally lured a vacationing Paramount star by paying fifty thousand dollars, double her normal salary: his *For the Love of Mike* star Claudette Colbert. Although Gable had shown up drunk for his first meeting with the director, Colbert pouted and threw tantrums, and his stars hated each other, Capra was working movie magic. Despite Colbert's complaint immediately after making the movie that it was "the worst picture in the world" (uttered, obviously, before the shower of Oscars), Capra produced an uninhibited, rollicking performance from the normally far more subdued actress. He wasn't modest about hogging the credit, either, later asserting that Gable's engaging performance was entirely due to his being allowed, for the first and only time, to play himself, a fun-loving, boyish rogue. And some of the success simply came, serendipitously, over the transom. When Colbert discovered that, because of her reluctance to hitch up her skirt, a double's leg was going to be used in the movie's hitchhiking scene, Colbert demanded to do the shot herself. The resulting shot became one of Hollywood's most famous images.

After the success of *It Happened One Night*, Capra entered his most creative as well as his most controversial period, evolving from a celebrated maker of witty, fast-moving films to an equally celebrated filmmaker preaching a personal sermon to his audience. It apparently came about because of a personal epiphany that weirdly presages the appearance of Clarence, the "second-class angel" in *It's a Wonderful Life*, made more than a decade later.

According to his memoirs, at about this time Capra lost his appetite and began experiencing night sweats and the "swarms" of migraine headaches that were to plague his retirement years. After three doctors failed to find anything wrong with him, Capra, who by then had lost thirty-four pounds and was convinced he was soon going to die, claims he received a mysterious visit from a "little man . . . completely bald, wearing thick glasses." The visitor told him that he (Capra) was a "coward" and "an offense to God." Hitler, the mysterious visitor said, could reach only 15 or 20 million people with his message of evil, while Capra could tell his stories of good overcoming evil and inhumanity to hundreds of millions. "God gave you those talents," Capra claims the man told him. "And when you don't use the gifts God blessed you with, you are an offense to God—and to humanity." Then the man left and Capra never saw him again.

Whether true or a hallucination, Capra says he was cured by the bizarre incident, got out of bed, and went back to work convinced that he must "say something" in his future films, films that he would later describe as sharing the theme of "a simple honest man, driven into a corner by predatory sophisticates, [who] can, if he will, reach down into his God-given resources and come up with the necessary handfuls of courage, wit, and love to triumph over his environment."

And, aside from at least one critic's observation that it was here that Capra crossed the line between populist entertainment and populist demagoguery, for the most part the "message" movies succeeded. The first of them was 1936's *Mr. Deeds Goes to Town*. After seriously considering following *It Happened One Night* with *Valley Forge*, a patriotic saga based on a book by Maxwell Anderson about George Washington's bleakest months in America's fight for freedom, Capra seized on a property called *Opera Hat*. Written by Clarence Buddington Kelland, the novel reflected the then popular theme of the unsophisticated hero versus the city folk; in this case, it was the story of an honest country boy named Longfellow Deeds from rural Mandrake Falls who inherits $20 million and an opera house and outwits everyone who wants a part of it. That it was made in the middle of the Great Depression didn't hurt the film's box office performance either, nor did Capra's obvious pandering to the American penchant of making a hero of the anti-intellectual. Deeds defends his profession of writing hokey jingles for greeting cards by saying, "It's easy to make fun of somebody if you don't care how much you hurt him. . . . I guess maybe it *is* comical to write poems for postcards, but a lot of people think they're good."

Gary Cooper was Capra's first and only choice for the character. "Every line in his face spelled honesty," Capra said. For his heroine, Babe Bennett, a reporter who tries to figure out why Deeds wants to give away his money, he was less sure until he heard, from the soundtrack of a film running in an adjoining projection room at Columbia, the low and husky voice of an actress that, when it broke into higher octaves, sounded "like a thousand tinkling bells."

Her name was Jean Arthur, and she was a former Broadway actress who had previously tried to break into films and failed; some may have considered her voice more squeaky than bell-like, but, thanks to Capra, she would become one of the era's best-loved comediennes. The movie won Capra a second Best Director Oscar and was the first—other than those made by directors such as D. W. Griffith, Cecil B. DeMille, and Chaplin when they owned their own companies—to feature the director's name above the title and stars of the film. The movie, like many of Capra's, would contribute new words to our dictionary, in this case "doodled" and "pixilated" (for happily drunk).

Before he got around to his most famous country-boy-versus-the-establishment picture, 1939's *Mr. Smith Goes to Washington*, Capra made two films that treated the theme a bit differently and have also endured as film classics, 1937's *Lost Horizon* and the following year's *You Can't Take It with You*.

It cost Harry Cohn two hundred thousand dollars (the most ever paid for a property at the time) to buy the rights for *You Can't Take It with You*, the George Kaufman/Moss Hart Pulitzer Prize–winning Broadway play about a happy-go-lucky family, and Capra shot 329,000 feet of film to make it (a finished feature picture then contained some eight thousand feet), but it was worth every penny. The cast, including Lionel Barrymore, Jean Arthur, Jimmy Stewart (first playing the role of an idealist who rejects his father's Wall Street patrimony), Spring Byington (who would receive an Oscar nomination for the supporting role of Penny Sycamore), Eddie Anderson (Jack Benny's radio deflator, Rochester), Edward Arnold, and Ann Miller, was probably the best you could assemble in Hollywood at the time. The film won Best Picture and Oscar number three for Capra. Ann Miller, the only member of the cast still alive, remembers the experience of working with Capra as a high point in a glittering career.

The second of these movies didn't win anything—except enduring cult fame. *Lost Horizon* was, from the start, a challenge, and one that nearly spelled *finis* to Capra's string of hits. It was based on James Hilton's novel about a Utopian paradise called Shangri-La hidden in Tibet, where for centuries the wisdom of the ages had been accumulated (and where, happily, no one ever grows old). Although Cohn was aghast at the estimated production cost of $2 million—two and a half times the studio's entire annual budget— he went along with it because, as the director remembers: "(I was) the hot crapshooter who had rolled four sevens in a row." Picking a lead was easy. Capra wanted only one person to play the sensitive intellectual kidnapped to carry on the dream of Shangri-La's dying High Lama of one day providing a resource of wisdom for a war-torn world: the sensitive, intellectual actor Ronald Colman.

Writing the script with his frequent colleague Robert Riskin at a desert hideaway was easier than figuring out how to re-create Tibet's ice-covered passes and Shangri-La's Edenlike Valley of the Blue Moon. Eventually, production demands required building miniatures, a full-size re-creation of the Art Deco lamasery, hiring an icehouse for six weeks of shooting the "cold" scenes, finding extras who could pass for Tibetans (Pala Indians from nearby San Diego), and dressing young steers in long-haired, hoof-length blankets so that they could pass as yaks. A young starlet named Jane Wyatt was cast as the romantic lead, and thirty-eight-year-old stage actor Sam Jaffe was found to play the two-century-old High Lama (Jaffe's weak voice, designed to convey his age in the film, prompted Capra to ban all carbonated beverages on the set when it was discovered that the microphones, adjusted to pick up Jaffe's whispered speech, also picked up the actors' and crew's gurgling stomachs).

Going into previews, Capra's biggest worry was not about the film's reception but how the first test audiences would react to the score of a Russian-born, ex–concert pianist named Dimitri Tiomkin whom Capra hired on a hunch. They liked the music but, to Capra's (and Cohn's) intense frustration, audiences laughed at the lines of the director's "poetic saga." After several days of worry, Capra decided on a radical move; he claims he threw away the first two reels of the film to get to the story faster (the early reels showed more of the revolution from which *Lost Horizon*'s characters were fleeing when they crashed in Tibet), and the film then "worked." Capra, again, was fibbing. It's true that he did burn (literally) the first two reels, but, as film historians discovered when *Lost Horizon* was reconstructed in the 1970s, the biggest cuts were made in the body of what remains; the original film, which ran nearly three hours, was pared to 132 minutes in its first release, then to 119 for the general release, and less than 100 minutes in the 1970s (it is now available in a 134-minute restored version with stills inserted where soundtrack but no images existed).

In attempting to explain the cool reception of *Lost Horizon*, Capra said: "Poetic sagas are dangerous. If audiences get a hint of what you are up to before they are 'conditioned' they may resent it and shy away. That's why films about Lincoln, about saints, about Christ, are dangerous. Actors begin wearing halos long before they have earned them." The movie also introduced the name Shangri-La to the language to designate a utopian site (the name apparently was derived by Hilton from Changri-La the name of a mountain pass in Tibet frequented by George Mallory, the legendary mountain climber who died on Mount Everest in 1924); Franklin D. Roosevelt and Harry S. Truman named the presidential retreat in Maryland's Catoctin Mountains Shangri-La. President Eisenhower later renamed it Camp David after his grandson.

Two of Capras next three films, more than any, account for his fame: 1940's *Mr. Smith Goes to Washington* and *It's a Wonderful Life*, made six years later after Capra left Columbia and formed his own production company.

Following the release of the 1940 film, one reviewer exclaimed, "I'd call *Mr. Smith Goes to Washington* just about the best American patriotic film ever made." That was clearly the intention of Capra when he read *The Gentleman from Montana*, an out-of-print book about a pet shop owner named Jefferson Smith who is picked by a corrupt political machine as a politically "safe" man to fill out an unexpired Senate term. And a great patriotic film was exactly what the Washington establishment expected from the now celebrated director when they turned out in droves for the premiere, sponsored by the National Press Club on October 3, 1939 ("Mr. Smith Day" in the nation's capital), in Constitution Hall. But it didn't work out quite that way. Despite advance reviews hailing *Mr. Smith* as one of the year's best films, the audience detested it for daring to show that graft was possible in the august halls of the U.S. Senate. According to Capra, maddest of all were members of the Washington press corps who felt they had been portrayed as a sorry lot of alcoholics. "Shifts of hopping mad Washington press correspondents belittled, berated, scorned, vilified, and ripped me open from stem to stern," Capra said of the party following the premiere. One, who could have been a character out of one of the director's own films, yelled, while juggling a martini: "There isn't one Washington correspondent in this room that drinks on duty or off duty."

Some of the reaction was understandable. The movie opened exactly a month after England and France had declared war on Nazi

Germany, and other war clouds were gathering around the world. It was hardly the time to satirize the government with a film about a hayseed senator with a crate of homing pigeons to send letters back home to Ma, and the naïveté to disrupt the Senate's deliberations with a filibuster during which he had the temerity to attack the honor of his state's senior senator. Some critics went so far as to claim Capra's film, by showing corruption in high places, was treasonous.

But tempers cooled, and supported by nearly unanimous rave reviews, the film began its rise to near universal popularity. No wonder. Jimmy Stewart and Jean Arthur were perfect to play the idealistic freshman senator, and the cynical secretary with, naturally, a heart of gold. For the hero-villain senior senator, Capra took a gamble on the British actor Claude Rains. To play the cynical, poet-quoting reporter Diz, Capra picked Thomas Mitchell, who had been struck by supporting-role lightning in 1939 and was on his way to becoming one of the most popular actors in Hollywood. In addition to appearing in Capra's movie (he earlier appeared in *Lost Horizon* and would star in both *It's a Wonderful Life* and Capra's final film, *A Pocketful of Miracles*), Mitchell also played Scarlett O'Hara's father in *Gone with the Wind* and appeared in *The Hunchback of Notre Dame* and Howard Hawks's *Only Angels Have Wings*; he won the Best Supporting Actor Oscar for John Ford's 1938 adventure, *The Hurricane*.

Mr. Smith ended Capra's contractual relationship with Cohn's Columbia, and when David Selznick, riding high on his success with *Gone with the Wind*, offered Capra an office at his studio, Capra accepted and mortgaged his house to finance his next project (he needed money since he had paid $240,000 in taxes that year on an income of $300,000, the second highest tax bill in Hollywood after Louis B. Mayer's). It was to be another "message" movie—this time about a drifter, used to defraud thousands by "forces of evil," who then tries to redeem himself by explaining that he's a fake—called *Meet John Doe*. Casting was easy: Gary Cooper as the hobo, and Barbara Stanwyck, Walter Brennan, Edward Arnold, and Spring Byington accepted key roles without even reading the script. They should have read it. For one thing, Capra, probably for the first and only time in his career, didn't know how to end the film and filmed four versions. "For seven-eighths of the film . . . I felt we had made The Great American Picture," he later reflected. "But in the last eighth it fizzled into The Great American Letdown." Most critics liked it, but the public was puzzled.

So Capra decided to make a quickie low-budget movie to redeem his injured finances, and it turned out to be one of his best: *Arsenic and Old Lace*. One reason was the script by the team of Jules and Philip Epstein, who in 1943 were to immortalize themselves with *Casablanca*. Cary Grant headed a wonderful cast, starring as Mortimer Brewster, the drama critic with a pair of eccentric aunts whose hobby is making lonely men happy by killing them. During filming, the Japanese attacked Pearl Harbor; after finishing and editing his film, Capra was inducted into the Army Signal Corps and ordered to Washington. Because of the war, *Arsenic and Old Lace* wasn't released until 1944 and, according to Capra, "made money so fast his first percentage check was for $232,000." Unfortunately, the tax bite was $205,000.

While in the army, Capra was assigned to the Signal Corps, where he made a series of propaganda documentaries called *Why We Fight,* generally considered the best such films of the era. For this service, Capra, a colonel when he was discharged, was awarded the Congressional Medal of Honor, America's highest decoration. Commenting on his role in articulating U.S. foreign policy through the series, Capra wrote: "Thus, it can truly be said that the *Why We Fight* films not only stated but, in many instances, actually created and nailed down American and world pre-war policy. No, I won't say it. Yes, I will say it. I was the first 'Voice of America.'"

When peace came, Capra's challenge was to figure out what kind of movie to make next. America had gone through the triumph and tragedy of war, and what it clearly didn't want was another "war" movie. But, like millions around the world, Capra could hardly have been untouched by the worldwide conflict, and, indeed, his next film is noticeably darker in tone than his earlier movies. In fact, some see it as a very angry film noir about death and loss and a small town battling capitalist overlords: *It's a Wonderful Life*. It was the first movie released by Capra's own independent studio, Liberty Films Company.

Centering around a loan company manager named George Bailey (James Stewart) who contemplates suicide and is shown in a nightmarish sequence how the lives of those close to him would have been changed for the worse had he never lived, the movie got mixed reviews when it opened, ranging from *Life*'s "a masterful edifice of comedy and sentiment" to the *New York Times*'s "a figment of simple Pollyanna platitudes." Perhaps they had in mind such treacley sentiments as one uttered by Clarence, the friendly angel: "Remember, no man is a failure who has friends."

Based on "The Greatest Gift," a story written as a Christmas gift by Philip van Doren Stern, it was, as Capra later recalled with, of course, the convenience of twenty-twenty hindsight "the kind of idea that when I get old and sick and scared and ready to die—they'll still say, 'He made *The Greatest Gift*.'" It would be, he added, "a film that said to the downtrodden, the pushed-around, the pauper . . . the disillusioned and the disheartened . . . to show to the slow of foot or slow of mind . . . each man's life touches so many other lives." Without reading the script, Lionel Barrymore, who plays the film's archetypical skinflint, requested a loan-out from MGM. For the female lead and the young, blonde sexpot, he got two additional MGM loan-outs whose careers were made by the film: Donna Reed and Gloria Grahame.

Although *It's a Wonderful Life* was nominated in three categories (Best Picture, Actor, and Director), it won in none, beaten out by William Wyler's poignant *The Best Years of Our Lives*. Until it was rediscovered (with a vengeance) by a later generation, the public was lukewarm to it. Despite President Harry Truman's enthusiasm for Capra's next film, the even darker *State of the Union*, in which Capra clearly has lost his optimism, the public didn't take to it, either. Forced to sell Liberty to Paramount, Capra said: "I fell never to rise to be the same man again either as a person or a talent. I lost my nerve . . . for fear of losing a few bucks."

He should have stopped then, at the top of his profession. But like actors who hold on until they become caricatures of themselves, Capra continued until his work was barely recognizable; he had lost more than his nerve; he had lost faith in his own sentimental view of society. As one observer said of Capra in a 1998 *Washington Post* feature: "He put all his faith in George Bailey and it turned out there were no George Baileys. He had nowhere to go, which is possibly why his postwar career was such a bust."

1950 brought *Riding High,* and the following year *Here Comes the Groom*, most memorable for Bing Crosby's rendition of "In the Cool, Cool, Cool of the Evening." Then silence until 1959's *A Hole in the Head*, an unconvincing comedy starring Frank Sinatra. Then the final *Pocketful of Miracles*.

In the title song of *A Pocketful of Miracles*, Frank Sinatra sings: "It's Christmas every day, life is a carousel, the world's a bright and shining apple that's mine, all mine."

For at least a generation, that was as good a description of Frank Capra's life and talent as any.

In 1910, when *The Wizard of Oz* author L. Frank Baum moved to Hollywood, citrus groves and vineyards (for which Vine Street was named) were everywhere. In 1923 there was still a large grove at the intersection of Lexington and Gower Streets owned by Senator Cornelius Cole, a former advisor to Abraham Lincoln who would die the following year at 101. Here he welcomes the fourteen-year-old Douglas Fairbanks, Jr., whose father, the legendary silent film swashbuckler, and stepmother Mary Pickford, then reigned as the "King and Queen of Hollywood."

The Lost Idyll—Subdividing Oz

In popular myth—especially during the early years of Hollywood's golden age—the image of Southern California was that of a bountiful paradise on earth. It was, at least in the mind of the celebrated author of the *Oz* books, L. Frank Baum, the embodiment of Oz itself, a never-never land of beauty and prosperity where he set all but the first of his celebrated series of fourteen books.

In 1910, six years after finding personal celebrity with *The Wonderful Wizard of Oz*, Baum moved with his wife, Maude, their four sons, and a red cocker spaniel (named, naturally, Toto) to Coronado Island, near San Diego. There, along with writing and engaging in his lifelong love of archery, he would design the crown-shaped chandeliers still hanging in the huge dining room of what attracted the couple to Coronado in the first place, the Hotel del Coronado, previously their favorite vacation site.

The following year, the Baums moved to Hollywood

and built a spacious home on a huge (100 by 183 feet) lot at 1749 Cherokee Street, a block north of Prospect (now Hollywood Boulevard), and named it Ozcot. And it was there, where he was working on *Glinda of Oz* in a library containing his famous file cabinet (the drawer labeled O-Z inspired the name of his utopia), Baum died in 1919. Today, more than eighty years later, Ozcot is gone, replaced by a community garden. Baum, for whom horticulture was more than a hobby—he won numerous first prizes for his flowers—would have been, one hopes, pleased.

The image of Los Angeles as a form of paradise was even more broadly—if inadvertently—evangelized by the silent films of the era. One silent film star said he moved to California from the east because, always seeing shadows in the movies of the time, he realized that the sun must always be shining.

Commercial interests motivated much of the promotion, too. It was the codependent relationship between the railroads and the Southern California citrus growers that, more than anything else, convinced America that the place must be a heaven on earth. The story was promulgated by some of the most aggressive advertising in history. A lot of it was hype—no place could be as good as claimed by the Chicago advertising agency hired by the growers association, the Automobile Association of America, the Los Angeles Chamber of Commerce (which for a time maintained a "California on Wheels" train that toured America promoting the area), and the Santa Fe and Southern Pacific Railroads themselves. But, energized by the dream, people kept coming because most of it *was* true. The beaches, lapped by the blue green waters of the Pacific, were indeed golden. The azure sky was, more often than not, cloudless, the air, in this presmog era, was healthy (especially important in a tuberculosis-plagued world), and it was all protectively embraced by snowcapped mountains in the far distance.

It all started with a fruit that, not only was emblematic of youth and beauty in Western culture but also was a visual embodiment of California's idealized sun itself: the orange.

Even though raising oranges was an established cottage industry in Florida early on, many Americans in 1900 had never seen an orange, much less tasted one. For that matter, neither had most of the world's population outside of the Indian subcontinent (where they apparently originated) and the Mediterranean countries where, at least in an ancient Greek creation myth, oranges were the "golden apples."

Introduced and established in Spain by the Arabs in the Middle Ages, oranges were first brought to the New World by Columbus on his second voyage in 1493. Eventually, they spread throughout much of Spain's New World empire, including Mexico, the Caribbean, Florida (where centuries later they would become the state's major agricultural crop), and, in 1739, Baja California.

It's more or less commonly known that the California wine industry began when the Franciscan monks, starting in 1769, established vineyards to supply sacramental wine as they built the celebrated chain of missions running north along the Camino Real from San Diego. Less well known is that in addition to their vines, the Franciscans introduced the orange to Southern California, first planting a six-acre grove in 1804 at the San Gabriel Mission. Then a trapper from Kentucky named William Wolfskill settled in what is now Los Angeles in 1841 and planted hundreds of orange and lemon seedlings (obtained from the mission) on two acres of land at Central Avenue and East Fifth Street, later the site of the Southern Pacific Central Station. By 1862, there were twenty-five thousand orange and lemon trees in the area, and twenty years later, more than half a million.

In 1870, just a year after the golden spike was driven at Promontory Point, Utah, to complete the transcontinental railroad, California oranges were first shipped to eastern markets from San Francisco, but the real boom came when the Santa Fe Railroad opened its route to Los Angeles in 1885. In February of the following year, an entire trainload of California's golden fruit arrived in the snowbound east; beginning in 1920, thirty thousand railroad cars filled with Valencia and Washington navel oranges, then and still the backbone of the industry, rolled eastward each year. That amounted to some twelve million orange crates, each of them decorated with labels portraying idealized visions of California rendered in the cartoon-intense colors of a Maxfield Parrish painting. Whenever and wherever one shopped, California's message was unmissable.

In 1904, one of the most famous American trademarks, Sunkist, came into general use; soon the name was stamped on each individual orange, lemon, and grapefruit produced by the California Fruit Growers Exchange. The exchange was then the quintessential example of the agricultural cooperative, made up of fifteen thousand citrus growers and two hundred packing associations. There were also dozens of citrus groves in Hollywood, although most were lemon; when the Baums settled on Cherokee Street, Maud Baum later recalled that orange trees lined the street. In 1900, 70 percent of America's lemons were imported from Italy; twenty years later, 85 percent came from California.

Today, of course, most of those groves have disappeared under real estate developments, shopping centers, and freeways. But, since citrus trees can live two or three hundred years (one of the parent grafts of the Washington navel orange still survives in Riverside, a city sixty miles east of Los Angeles founded in 1887, thirteen years after the tree was planted), it's not surprising that a few gnarled examples can be found here and there. A hundred miles south of Hollywood, in the rarified surroundings of Rancho Santa Fe, whole groves of citrus still cover the hillsides.

By the turn of the twentieth century, it was clear that if growth were to continue in what was essentially a semiarid desert, a greater supply of water was necessary (the population of Los Angeles county, 170,000 in 1900, would jump to 500,000 in 1910 and by 1920, 936,000). This wasn't exactly a new idea; in fact, as early as 1868, a system of reservoirs and irrigation ditches was established to augment the unpredictable supply drawn from the Los Angeles River. The story of what happened next has inspired all sorts of tales told from all sorts of political viewpoints, perhaps the most famous being Roman Polanski's film *Chinatown*, in which writer Robert Towne fictionalized elements of a related incident that took place a generation later. But, the original happenings were as good or better than any movie, involving deceit and daring, all tangled together as intimately as in a film plot.

While camping by the Owens River (east of the Sierra Nevada, some two hundred miles north of Los Angeles) in 1892, LA's former city engineer and future mayor, Fred Eaton, seized on the idea of diverting the river's destination from the brackish Owens Lake into an aqueduct that would serve his city's growing needs. Eaton's idea would soon become one of the greatest engineering feats in U.S. history, take years to complete, and raise passions that have not entirely died even today, more than a century later.

To make it happen, the Los Angeles water supply had to be municipalized so that a bond issue could be floated to finance the acqueduct, the Owens Valley land had to be removed from the public domain, and an engineer had to be found to spearhead the effort. By 1904, when Eaton chose the new chief engineer of the municipalized water company and took him on a buckboard trip to the Owens Valley following the potential route of the aqueduct, all had been set in motion. Eaton's companion, an Irish immigrant who first supported himself after arriving in Los Angeles in 1877 at the age of twenty-two by digging some of those early irrigation ditches, would, for posterity, be portrayed as both an enlightened engineer and as a fellow conspirator of the developers who needed the water. His name was William Mulholland. In his defense, without the Owens Valley water, which could supply the needs of 2 million residents, ten times the population of the time, Los Angeles could never have become one of the great cities of the world. But history also looks on Mulholland, who died in July 1935, as the man who destroyed the idyllic, agricultural Owens Valley by stealing its water and making millions of dollars for his friends when the aqueduct made possible the development of thousands of acres of hitherto worthless land.

All the negotiations with the city were done in secret and all local newspapers but one backed the scare tactics linking failure to build the acqueduct to economic collapse predicted by Mulholland to secure the money needed from the public coffers (a total of $27 million over the six years it took to complete the project, the equivalent of a third of a billion dollars today). That one renegade paper was William Randolph Hearst's *Examiner*, which blew the whistle on the whole deal, revealing that the publishers of his two major rivals (the *Times* and the *Express*) were part of a syndicate that was buying up thousands of acres in the San Fernando Valley. The value of the semi-desert land clearly would soar once the aqueduct was completed; other members of the syndicate, known as the San Fernando Mission Land Company (nothing particularly subtle about these folks) included Henry Huntington of the Pacific Electric Railroad, E. H. Harriman, whose Union Pacific Railroad controlled the Southern Pacific, the Security Trust and Savings Bank, and, somewhat embarrassingly, the city's water commissioner, Moses Sherman.

Then, within only weeks, Hearst backed down by way of an editorial in his paper endorsing the bond issue. What happened? No one knows for certain, but the best guess is that the newspaper-owning syndicate members bought off Hearst, then a congressman from New York planning a run for the presidency, by agreeing to back his candidacy. So the bond measure passed and, lobbied by Mulholland, the U.S. government dropped all reclamation claims to the Owens Valley. President Theodore Roosevelt then declared much of the valley a federal forest reserve, thus precluding homesteading and creating a right of way for the aqueduct. Before construction, the route into Los Angeles was changed to include three major drops in the aqueduct where enough electricity could be generated to serve the needs of the city as well as Pasadena, Santa Monica, and the LA harbor area. The decision was the genesis of LA's soon to be notoriously all-powerful Department of Water and Power.

To bring it off took a remarkable amount of planning. Two hydroelectric plants anchoring 169 miles of lines had to be built in the Owens Valley just to supply the electric power needed to build the project, and, because so much cement was required, the city had to build a plant where 250 workmen mixed a special formula devised by Mulholland. In addition, 250 miles of telephone lines had to be run; a railroad had to be laid through the Mojave Desert; 500 miles of roads had to be constructed; 50 miles of tunnels blasted out of rock, and more than two thousand tents bought to house a movable village of hundreds of (nonunion) workers. The work started in 1907 and took six years to complete, with every moment overseen by Mulholland, who rode up and down the line, prodding and inspiring his workers to ever greater efforts, all the while keeping the project on budget. One defining story was related by California historian Kevin Starr: When a tunnel worker was trapped by a cave-in, he stayed alive until rescued by eating hard-boiled eggs rolled down a conduit; Mulholland later suggested that he be charged for the food.

Finally it was done. On the morning of November 5, 1913, a

crowd of some forty thousand gathered at the base of the spillway in the northern reaches of the San Fernando Valley for the dedication of the aqueduct that would be signaled by the opening of the final spillway. Mulholland made a short speech, ending with his terse, often quoted remark, "There it is. Take it." Most of the crowd did, surging forward to taste the newly arrived water from the Owens River in tin cups that they brought along for the event.

Mulholland lived eighty-seven years, watching his reputation deteriorate for the last twenty years of his life as Los Angeles had to pay for debt service on bonds sold to finance a water supply it didn't yet need. Worse, on March 12, 1928, the Mulholland-designed St. Francis Dam along the route collapsed, releasing 11.4 billion gallons of water and drowning 450 people; it was one of the worst peacetime disasters in U.S. history. Although Mulholland first claimed at the inquest that followed that irate Owens Valley ranchers had dynamited the dam, it was soon established that the structure had been leaking badly at its base before the collapse, a warning that Mulholland dismissed as normal. Eventually he accepted responsibility with the words "I envy the dead."

The aqueduct made possible the development of thousands of acres of land in the San Fernando Valley, much of it owned by the syndicate which made millions, but Mulholland, still often portrayed by posterity as a crook and a murderer, didn't make a cent. When the San Fernando Valley was annexed in 1915, it doubled the size of Los Angeles and enabled the city's huge growth in the 1920s.

Hollywood has always promoted its creations aggressively, but rarely over as long a period as the development of the San Fernando Valley. In 1943—thirty years after water first arrived—songwriter Gordon Jenkins, who would later go on to arrange the hits "My Foolish Heart," "Bewitched, Bothered and Bewildered," "Goodnight, Irene," and "So Long, It's Been Good to Know Ya," composed a song deliberately written to promote living in the valley. Recorded first by Roy Rogers (who starred in the film of the same name in 1944), the song "San Fernando Valley," became a number-one hit when recorded that year by Bing Crosby (who owned thousands of acres in the Valley). Many older residents of Los Angeles still wince at the memory of the saccharine song, played to distraction in its time. But there is little question that it contributed substantially to the postwar rush of the hundreds of thousands of people to Southern California by portraying the area in terms clearly designed to appeal to Americans eager to move on after the sacrifices of the war years:

> *"Oh! I'm packing my grip,*
> *and I'm leaving today*
> *'Cause I'm taking a trip California way.*
>
> *I'm gonna settle down and never more roam*
> *And make the San Fernando Valley my home."*

To most of this new generation of California immigrants, the prospect of buying a home for ten dollars down and fifty dollars a month, buying gasoline for 10.9 cents per gallon, never having to shovel snow, and picking oranges off a tree in the backyard, probably seemed like paradise.

The San Fernando Valley was never idyllic. And neither was Baum's Southern California or Hollywood, unless one viewed it through the emerald-colored glasses needed by his *Wizard of Oz* characters to avoid being blinded by the beauty of the city. But for several generations it seemed to be.

Perhaps that was enough.

A star at the age of seven, Bobby Driscoll won a special Oscar when he was fourteen, and co-starred in more than thirty films. But he was also a drug addict by the time he was seventeen. Here in 1961 he is shown being transferred in handcuffs from the Los Angeles County Jail to a state drug rehabilitation facility. It did little good; Bobby was found dead in a New York flophouse seven years later.

Getting High in Hollywood

Drugs and alcohol have been the flip side of Hollywood fame from the beginning. Throughout film history, some actors and actresses have been seriously addicted to drugs; many have also used drugs infrequently or not at all until, desperate over personal or professional setbacks, they reached for the bottle. It was J. Edgar Hoover's relentless pursuit of Jean Seberg, because of her friendship with leaders of the Black Panther movement in the 1960s, that caused her, in 1979, to seek peace through Seconal. (Hoover's FBI had deliberately spread the lie that she had become pregnant by a Panther, forcing Seberg to bury her baby—who died soon after birth—in a glass casket so that all could see it was white.) But whether the use was "recreational," occasional, or terminal, the result was the same . . . a loss to the film industry and movie fans that can never be measured.

In June 1941, playwright Bertolt Brecht arrived from

Germany and, after living in Hollywood for a short time, rented a small house on Twenty-fifth Street in Santa Monica for $48.50 per month. It wasn't long before he was referring to Los Angeles as "the world capital of the narcotics trade." Long before Brecht's arrival—in fact, from the very beginnings of the film industry—drugs, like sex, were part of the Hollywood lifestyle. With the mention of drugs, most film fans can summon a list of high-profile actors who have died—sometimes inadvertently—from overdoses or overuse: Marilyn Monroe and, of course, Judy Garland, whose career and life were eventually destroyed by a drug addiction she blamed on Louis B. Mayer, who she claimed looked the other way when the MGM doctor fed her speed to keep her weight down during the making of the *Andy Hardy* series. But there have been many more stars, each potentially another Monroe or Garland, whose lives were cut short before their potential was realized. And their stories are just as gripping—and just as tragic—as those of their more famous colleagues.

In 1920, silent film star Olive Thomas, considered the most beautiful girl in the world, died in Paris of an overdose while awaiting the arrival of her actor husband, Jack Pickford, for a belated honeymoon. Pickford, a drug addict himself, was the younger brother of America's Sweetheart and the most powerful actor in Hollywood, Mary Pickford. Two years later, Wallace Reid, one of Hollywood's most popular actors, died of an overdose in an asylum. And, although the murder has never been solved, the famous Mabel Normand, mistress of Mack Sennett and costar of Chaplin, was, because of her cocaine addiction, probably involved in one of the silent era's most sensational unsolved crimes, the 1921 murder of director William Desmond Taylor.

Scandals like these helped bring on Hollywood's self-censorship in the form of the Hays Commission, established in the early 1920s and headed by President Harding's Postmaster General Will Hays. But his austere presence had little effect on drug use in the film capital other than eventually bringing on a wave of "instructional" antidrug propaganda films. Among such unintentionally humorous efforts such as *Devil's Madness* and *Marijuana, the Weed with Roots in Hell*, was 1936's *Reefer Madness*, a movie that portrayed marijuana-addicted teens as toked-up zombies stumbling through situations so contrived, they make films by horror schlockmeister Roger Corman seem positively Shakespearian. The film, so hysterically bad that it is now a cult classic, actually spawned an award-winning musical that debuted in 1999 at the Hudson Theatre in—natch'—Hollywood, before moving on to New York.

There is a difference, however, between drug use in Hollywood's golden age and today. Then, like most of what really went on in Hollywood behind the cameras, the common use of drugs was largely a secret to the moviegoing public. Sometimes the effort to keep a habit hidden was even amusing. Carmen Miranda, she of the swirling skirts and banana-topped hats, known in the 1940s as the Brazilian bombshell, kept her stash of coke handy but hidden in her famous platform shoes.

Because drugs can be so lethal, their use in Hollywood has been inevitably linked with suicides. But it's not always easy to know whether a suicide is the result of a one-time overdose of, say, Seconal, an accident, or an outgrowth of an addiction. Compared to jumpers or those who hang or shoot or drown or gas themselves, not many people leave notes before deliberately killing themselves with an overdose. The betting is, however, that suicide by drug overdose is more often than not committed by someone with more than a passing familiarity with drugs. Many golden era deaths from drugs—deliberate or not—add a deeper understanding of the work climate in Hollywood at the time. Drugs, including alcohol, provide an escape from reality, and whether protected by a contract or not, the pressure of making it in Hollywood—and then staying on top—is unrelenting, often cruel and unfair, and certainly capricious.

Take the case of Jeanne Eagels. In 1927, Eagels, a luminously beautiful, blonde, thirty-four-year-old Jazz-Age carnival dancer and Broadway star from Kansas City, Missouri, arrived in Hollywood. Along with the fame she brought with her, gained from her portrayal of Sadie Thompson in a theatrical production of Somerset Maugham's *Rain* that took New York by storm several years earlier, Eagels also brought along a severe addiction to drugs and alcohol. Despite it and despite her constant severe bouts with depression, she made three films for MGM, receiving an Academy Award nomination for *The Letter* in 1929 before dying of a heroin overdose.

Was it suicide or an accident caused by anxiety over the challenge of sound? Or was it the loss of her money in the stock market crash? Or was it anxiety over her Academy Award nomination? Eagels, whose oft-quoted motto was "Never deny. Never explain. Say nothing and become a legend" was as good as her word and left no note. She died three months before she would know if she had won the Oscar or not (she didn't). Ironically, the legendary Hollywood status Jeanne Eagels dreamed of would be achieved—more or less—by another blonde actress who landed a *Time* magazine cover by portraying Eagels in a 1957 semifictionalized film biography: Kim Novak.

And then there is the case of John Gilbert, whose career was essentially destroyed by sound. He died, it was reported, of a heart attack in 1936, but there is little question that the longtime alcoholic drank himself to death because, as reflected in a plaintive ad he placed looking for work in *Variety* a couple of years earlier, nobody wanted him anymore.

In the 1940s, Lupe Velez made a series of films as the "Mexican Spitfire", earning herself a nickname that still endures. After breaking into films in 1926, she embarked on a number of affairs and marriages that never could have been imagined in her San Antonio, Texas, convent upbringing: Her paramours included John Gilbert and, most famously, Gary Cooper. In 1933 she married Tarzan himself, Johnny Weissmuller, and after their divorce had a series of lovers who diminished in stature as dramatically as her career and her savings.

In 1944, broke and pregnant by her last lover, Harald Raymond, she decided to kill herself and to do it with style, filling her home with masses of tuberoses and gardenias and inviting two close girlfriends for a Last Supper. After they left Velez, still dressed in her silver lamé gown, wrote a farewell note and, surrounded by dozen of lit candles, downed a bottle of Seconal tablets and lay back, her hands clasped in prayer, waiting for nature to take its course. Unfortunately, nature *did* take its course, but not in the way she expected. Her stomach rebelled before the sleeping pills kicked in, and she began vomiting her dinner as well as the sleeping pills, a reaction that should have saved her life. But, rushing into the bathroom, Velez slipped in her vomit on the tile floor, hit her head on the toilet, and died of a broken neck. It tends to make one believe in predestination.

And there is the story of Bobby Driscoll, a star at seven, winner of a special Academy Award at fourteen, costar with many of Hollywood's greatest in thirty films, a drug addict at seventeen, and dead in an unmarked grave at thirty-one. His sad saga could be a Cliffs Notes for what drugs can do.

Bobby was born in Cedar Rapids, Iowa, on May 7, 1937, and if it weren't for a move to Pasadena, California, by the family seeking a cure for his father's sinus condition, the silver screen would probably never have found him. Because of the enthusiasm of the son of their barber, William Kadel, who believed Bobby was perfect for playing a child in the many sentimental movies of the time, he was taken to an open interview at the MGM studios and immediately cast in a small, uncredited role in *Lost Angel* (1943).

Until 1946, Bobby played minor roles in such films as *From This Day Forward* (starring Joan Fontaine) and *O.S.S.* (with Alan Ladd). Then lightning struck when he was signed as Disney's first contract actor (all Disney films had, hitherto, been animated) and cast as Johnny in *Song of the South*. Playing the plantation boy who clung onto every word Uncle Remus spoke, Bobby delivered his role flawlessly; because of his performance and the financial success of the film, it was clear that Walt Disney had picked a winner.

Bobby went on to turn in notable film performances including 1948's *Melody Time* (with Roy Rogers), *So Dear to My Heart* (1949, with Burl Ives), and then, on loan to RKO, he was cast as a frightened little boy in *The Window*. In it, Driscoll's skill in portraying a child who has cried wolf too often for anyone to believe him when he actually witnesses a murder astounded everyone and gained him a special Best Child Oscar for his performance; there were those who believed he should have won Best Actor for this film.

The next year, Driscoll made the movie by which he is probably best remembered, *Treasure Island*. One of the most vivid memories of young moviegoers of that era was the sight of a terrified Bobby Driscoll shooting a murderous pirate right between the eyes; in fact, it was *so* vivid that the scene was cut when *Treasure Island* was reissued in the 1980s so that the film, which had been passed and approved by the 1950 censors, could qualify for a G rating. His last work for Disney was as the voice of Peter Pan in the 1953 animated film version of the beloved story (he also acted the role that was filmed and then rotoscoped for animation). Then, despite the fact that everyone at the studio sang his praises, he was dropped by Uncle Walt; the reason was simple and, like many in Hollywood, based solely on business. Driscoll was hired as a child actor; now at seventeen, he was no longer a child.

Two years later, Bobby got married and eventually had three children, but the path for the rest of his short life was set when he and a friend were arrested at his Pacific Palisades home on felony narcotics charges. In 1958, Driscoll made a turgid juvenile delinquent melodrama called *The Party Crashers* in which he starred with Frances Farmer, another doomed actor. Farmer, a Garbo look-alike leading lady of the 1930s, had been brutalized and raped during a seven-year treatment for manic-depressive psychosis culminating in a lobotomy performed with an ice pick (her story was told in the 1982 film *Frances* starring Jessica Lange). *The Party Crashers* was the last film for both.

Driscoll's drug problems continued. In 1960, he was booked for assault with a deadly weapon, and the following year he was arrested twice, once for robbing an animal clinic for drug money and then for forging a stolen check and for several narcotics charges. Before being sentenced to six months at the Narcotics Rehabilitation Center at the men's state prison in Chino, California, he told the court: "I had everything . . . I was earning more than fifty thousand dollars a year, and working steadily with good parts. Then I started putting all my spare time in my arm. I was seventeen when I first experimented with the stuff—mostly heroin, because I had the money to pay for it—and now no one will hire me because of my arrests." He had earlier said of his career: "They carried me on a satin pillow, then dumped me in the garbage."

After his release, Bobby moved to New York to try stage work, reportedly telling Jackie Cooper (who preceded Bobby as *Treasure Island*'s Jim Hawkins in the 1934 version of the story) that he just wanted to prove to the world that he really was a legitimate actor. Then he dropped out of sight.

On March 30, 1968, two children discovered the corpse of a young man, surrounded by religious objects and trash, in a deserted tenement off Avenue A in lower Manhattan. There was no identification on the corpse, but there were drug tracks on the arms and Methadrine in the blood. After being finger-printed, the body was buried in Potters Field on Hart Island, off the Bronx.

Nineteen months later, the Disney studio received a frantic call from Bobby's mother, explaining she had no idea where Bobby was but that his father was dying and wanted to see him. Eventually a fingerprint check disclosed that the unknown body buried in the pauper's grave was Bobby's; his father died two weeks before the body was found.

In *Song of the South*, James Baskett, who plays Uncle Remus, counsels Driscoll's Johnny with the words "You can't run away from trouble—there ain't no place that far." But Bobby wasn't listening when he made the movie, and in 1972, he wasn't listening anymore.

Peter Pan was dead.

Today most film fans remember only (and inaccurately) the gory details of Jayne Mansfield's death, little realizing how famous the one-time "Miss Tomato" was in the 1950s and 1960s. Here, outside their all-pink Los Angeles mansion, she and her husband, former Mr. Universe Mickey Hargitay, pose by their heart-shaped pool bearing an underwater sentiment from Hargitay inlaid in gold mosaic.

Bombshells—Blonde, Brash, and *Built*

While watching an early silent film recently, a friend remarked, "I can't believe they got away with all that nudity." They did. Even when compared with today's anything-goes license, the sheer acreage of naked flesh exploited in many early films is still astonishing. It was, of course, too good to last, ending with the imposition of self-censorship after a series of sex and drug scandals rocked the industry to its roots in the early 1920s. Like Prohibition, which it closely paralleled, Hollywood's new Victorianism would last almost exactly thirteen years. The ban on drinking required several million votes to finally repeal it, but bringing sex back to movies took only one man. Born in Los Angeles in 1895, William Berkeley Enos will always be remembered as Busby Berkeley.

In a string of musical extravaganzas including 1933's *42nd Street* and a series of annual *Gold Diggers* films, Berkeley liberated the Hollywood musical from the stage-bound with dazzling effects that included shooting from angles no director before had dreamed of. With technical skills that tantalized as well as delighted audiences by, among other tricks, shooting ranks of girls' legs as kinetic sculptures, dollying in, under, and through endless arches of thighs, and shooting from high above spectacularly choreographed *pas des milles* that could resemble water-lily vaginas opening and closing, Berkeley also peeled off the industry's blue stockings. Despite a somewhat unsettling penchant for violence (in *Gold Diggers of 1935*, the heroine falls screaming from a skyscraper; in *42nd Street*, there is a shooting and a stabbing during a production number) and the kinky (in *Small Town Girl*, Ann Miller dances among disembodied men's arms), Berkeley's perception of the audience's repressed lust for lasciviousness was clear, and his brilliance in satisfying it saved Warner Brothers from Depression-era bankruptcy and changed film forever.

Berkeley moved to MGM in 1939. But even then, housed at the prim studio that so desexualized the popular teen team of Mickey Rooney and Judy Garland that one could never imagine them getting to first base (or even knowing where the ballpark *was*), his innovations could still startle—take a look at the seemingly endless parade of erect bananas at the close of 1943's *The Gang's All Here*. But most of it was done so merrily that even the most prudish viewers could get so caught up in the spectacle that they rarely worried about the deeper meanings. Darryl Zanuck, head of production of Twentieth Century Fox from 1935 to 1952 and later president of the studio, saw it in simpler, more straightforward terms; to him it was all just "tit stuff."

Berkeley cleared a path for the arrival of the sex queen. And with a few exceptions (such as the raven-haired Rita Hayworth) they were—thanks to nature, chemistry, or the wig maker's art—blonde, brash, and *built*. Why blondes? As Anita Loos wrote in her sensationally popular 1925 play *Gentlemen Prefer Blondes*, "Gentlemen always seem to *remember* blondes." Despite the presence of the sensationally sculptured brunette Jane Russell in the 1953 film of the musical based on Loos's play, it's the platinum-blonde Marilyn Monroe one most remembers. Maybe *everybody* prefers blondes.

No social change happens in a vacuum, and a bit before Berkeley combined sex and effects with such stunning results, one woman had already begun to ride an image of indolent carnality to fame. Harlean Carpentier was born in Kansas City, Missouri, in 1911, where her childhood was strict but fairly normal. Harlean didn't know her own name until she entered private school—she was always called Baby by her family and the nickname stuck throughout her career. When her parents divorced, Harlean moved to Hollywood with her mother, a stereotypical stage mom who was determined that her daughter would fulfill her own frustrated film ambitions. But it was not to happen—yet. Harlean's mother, later well known as Mama Jean, soon married a failed Chicago entrepreneur named Mariano Bello. She and her daughter moved to Chicago and Harlean attended high school there for a time. Books were not for her, though, and when she was sixteen Harlean eloped with Charles McGraw, the twenty-one-year-old son of a local millionaire. The marriage was soon annulled and, with her mother and new stepfather, Harlean returned to Hollywood to break into movies. It didn't take long.

Two things happened quickly. Harlean met producer Hal Roach, who immediately put her into a few Laurel and Hardy films and got her first substantial role in Paramount's *The Saturday Night Kid*, starring the "It" girl, Clara Bow. And she changed her name to Jean Harlow.

The twenty-four-year-old Howard Hughes walked into Harlow's life in 1930 while she was working as an extra in Charlie Chaplin's *City Lights*. Hughes, who had already made a fortune in the Oklahoma oil fields and was using it to make movies, had just completed producing and directing *Hell's Angels*, a World War I epic. Because he had misjudged how quickly sound would take over the industry, the movie was silent and therefore unreleasable. So Hughes decided to reshoot it with a soundtrack. His star, the Swedish Greta Nissen, wouldn't do for the remake—her voice was too accented—so she suggested her friend Jean Harlow, who auditioned and got the part.

Hell's Angels made Harlow an overnight star, and it made Hughes even richer when he subsequently rented her out to other studios for movies such as Columbia's *Platinum Blonde* (1931). Under Frank Capra's direction, Harlow's screen persona as a languidly sexual and somewhat slatternly broad with a fast tongue was immortalized.

Her wisecracking directness and hearty good humor was a breath of fresh air in the middle of the Great Depression, and her disdain for underwear was both a liberating call to thousands of young women and a well-calculated publicity gambit (her comment "A brassiere is an unnecessary garment, actually unhealthy" sent the lingerie industry into a tailspin). Less fortunate was the impact of Harlow's famous platinum-blonde hair; trying to emulate the look with the caustic chemicals of the time caused thousands to go temporarily bald. In 1932, Hughes sold Harlow's contract to MGM, reserving the right to produce one more picture with her (it would be one of her best, 1933's *Bombshell*); the move soon brought the roaring lion a rare rebuke from Will Hays, the industry censor, for allowing Harlow's screen adultery in 1933's *Red-Headed Woman* to go unpunished.

Hell's Angels also marked the beginning of six years of enormous fame for Harlow, during which she made such classic films as 1931's *Public Enemy* (with its famous scene of James Cagney grinding a grapefruit half in her face) and 1932's *Red Dust* with Clark Gable, a sexually dynamic pairing that was repeated the following year in *Hold Your Man*. There followed such blockbusters as *China Seas, Dinner at Eight, Reckless*, and the appropriately titled *The Girl from Missouri*, in which she costarred with William Powell, the love of her last years. But she was always controversial, particularly to the older generation. On one famous occasion she was seated next to Margot Asquith, wife of the British prime minister at a Hollywood dinner party. After Harlow had mispronounced her name several times, Asquith turned to the actress and said, "My dear, the final 't' of 'Margot' is silent . . . just like 'Harlow.'"

On July 2, 1932, Harlow married one of her MGM producers, Paul Bern, who two months later killed himself in their bedroom with a .38 pistol. In his suicide note, he explained it was the only way "to make good the frightful wrong I have done you and wipe out my abject humiliation"; apparently a reference to his impotence. Further investigation turned up the fact that after Harlow's wedding night discovery that Bern's penis was as small as a child's and that he expected her to do something about it, he flew into a rage and beat her unconscious with a cane. The beating damaged her kidneys, and she never completely recovered.

After Bern's death, Harlow married a cameraman, but it lasted only eight months before she moved in with her mother and Bello, who were by then managing her career. They were, in fact, destroying it; in 1936, Louis B. Mayer responded to Bello's demand for more money for Harlow by suspending her.

During the filming of *Saratoga* in 1937, Harlow, whose drinking and drug use were becoming more of a problem, became ill and collapsed in costar Clark Gable's arms. But instead of allowing her to go to the hospital, her mother, a devout Christian Scientist, decided to treat the star herself, largely by reading tracts from Mary Baker Eddy's *Science and Health*, and refused to let anyone see her. By the time her ex-agent discovered how ill Harlow was, it was too late; she was suffering from inflammation of the gall bladder, and the infection had spread throughout her body before he was able to get her into a hospital. She died on June 7, 1937, at the age of twenty-six.

Harlow's Christian Science funeral at the chapel at Glendale's Forest Lawn Cemetery was a big one. MGM closed the studio for a day and all of the other studios observed a minute of silence. At the service Nelson Eddy sang "Ah Sweet Mystery of Life," and his film partner Jeanette MacDonald sang "Indian Love Call." Harlow was entombed in a twenty-five-thousand-dollar marble-lined private room (paid for by Powell) at the cemetery in a bronze and silver casket lined in pink silk and wearing the gown designed for her performance in the previous year's *Libeled Lady*, a not-to-be-missed, delightfully madcap film in which she costarred with Myrna Loy, Spencer Tracy, and her lover, William Powell. The film says more about how much Hollywood lost with the death of Jean Harlow than did any obituary.

As popular as she was, Jean Harlow lived a little early to be honored with the ultimate accolade paid to feminine beauty in the 1940s—becoming a pinup girl.

But Betty Grable became the most famous pinup girl of World War II. Her famous over-the-shoulder, come-hither photograph was pinned on barracks walls and tucked in the footlockers of more than one and a half million GI's. Her fresh-faced, all-

American-girl-next-door look was the very embodiment of What We Were Fighting For (and those legs, aggressively displayed in the photograph and famously insured for $1 million by Lloyds of London, certainly didn't hurt her popularity).

Betty Grable's career was also a perfect example of being in the right place at the right time. Born Ruth Elizabeth Grable in St. Louis on December 18, 1916, she was groomed from the start by her mother, Lillian, for a show business career. Dancing lessons were followed by singing lessons and, in 1929, a move to Hollywood where she was enrolled in dancing and acting classes and, eventually, in the Hollywood Professional School, started in 1935 to answer Louis B. Mayer's wish for a school that could cater to the flexible work schedule of Judy Garland. The school enrolled many stars, including Natalie Wood, Andy Williams, and Donald O'Connor, until it closed in 1985; its site at the corner of Sunset Boulevard and Serrano Street is now a supermarket parking lot.

Despite landing some jobs, nothing seemed to work for Grable; after making her debut (in blackface) in Busby Berkeley's first major film, 1930's *Whoopee*, she was saddled by B musicals, college campus movies such as *Pigskin Parade* and *The Sweetheart of Sigma Chi*, and singing with a local dance band. RKO, which had signed her after seeing her dance routine in the Fred Astaire/Ginger Rogers film *The Gay Divorcee*, dropped her contract; then Paramount, which also seemed not to know what to do with her, signed and dropped her after a half dozen unmemorable films. By then, though, Grable had become a household name, not for any movie she made but because of her relationship with Jackie Coogan, who at the age of six had made the world weep in Charlie Chaplin's 1921 movie *The Kid*. In 1938, the couple married, but it was an ill-fated union from the beginning, fractured by arguments over Coogan's squandering of Grable's income and his lawsuit over his parents' mishandling of his estimated $4 million income as a child actor (he got half of the $252,000 that remained; the 1939 California law that resulted, known as the Coogan Law, still protects child actors' earnings). The couple divorced in 1941.

In 1939, Fox's Daryl Zanuck, who had seen some of Grable's Paramount films, offered her a contract. Since he had nothing specific in mind, he first released her to work with Ethel Merman and Bert Lahr on Broadway's *DuBarry Was a Lady* but soon called her back to fill in for the ailing Alice Faye and costar with Don Ameche on the Technicolor musical extravaganza *Down Argentine Way*, Carmen Miranda's debut. Before the film was released, Zanuck put her to work again, costarring with the now recovered Faye in *Tin Pan Alley*, followed by a series of Technicolor musicals that entranced audiences everywhere—among them *Moon over Miami* (1941), *Springtime in the Rockies* (1942), and *Sweet Rosie O'Grady* (1943). While making *Springtime in the Rockies* with Cesar Romero and Carmen Miranda in 1942, she and Harry James, whose orchestra was featured in the film, became romantically attached. They married in Las Vegas on July 5 of the following year, but there was no time for a honeymoon—she had to start filming *Pin-Up Girl* (in which the pinup girl plays a pinup girl with too many fiancées). Their daughter, Victoria Elizabeth arrived the following March. (A second daughter, Jessica, arrived in May 1947.)

Grable was then at the height of her popularity, reinforced with the release of *Billy Rose's Diamond Horseshoe* (costarring Dick Haymes and Phil Silvers) in 1945, followed by *The Dolly Sisters*, another hit from which her only commercial recording originated: Although Fox prohibited its stars from working for recording companies, she recorded "I Can't Begin to Tell You" with the Harry James band under the pseudonym Ruth (her middle name) Haag (Harry James's mother's middle name).

For some reason, Zanuck decided his star who had parlayed a talent for making musicals into becoming the number-one box office star in America should be seen in heavier roles and offered her the female lead starring opposite Tyrone Power in the film version of Somerset Maugham's *The Razor's Edge*. Grable refused ("I'm a song and dance girl," she logically said), and Gene Tierney got the part. After making *Mother Wore Tights*, a very successful film and the first of four pairings with Dan Daily, she made the semiserious musical *That Lady in Ermine* in 1948, which also starred Douglas Fairbanks Jr., toward the close of his film career. The film was not a success, notable mainly for being the great director Ernst Lubitsch's final effort; he died of a heart attack seven days into filming and was replaced by Otto Preminger. Although more hits were to come (*When My Baby Smiles with Me, Wabash Avenue,* a remake of her 1943 film *Coney Island, My Blue Heaven*), the writing was clearly on the wall when Zanuck signed Mitzi Gaynor as part of his plan to ease Grable out.

It took four years and three suspensions—two for refusing to work because she was exhausted by making strenuous song-and-dance films back-to-back and one for refusing to be lent out to another studio—but after costarring with Marilyn Monroe and Lauren Bacall in 1952's *How to Marry a Millionaire,* she walked into Zanuck's office, tore up her contract, and said: "I'm leaving." (Ironically, when *Millionaire* was released in November 1953, it was Grable who got the best notices.) She made one more film for Fox: 1955's *How to Be Very, Very Popular.* Marilyn Monroe had turned it down; Grable should have also.

Like many actors who leave Hollywood, Betty Grable hit the television, nightclub, and road show circuits. The live audiences loved her, and when she and Dan Daily costarred in a production of *Guys and Dolls* at the Dunes Hotel in Las Vegas in December

1962, it was standing room only, as it was across America when she later toured in *Hello Dolly!*

But problems were piling up. In 1965, her twenty-year marriage to James ended amid rumors that he had gone through all her money. In 1972, while presenting the Oscar for Best Musical Score with Dick Haymes at the Academy Awards, Grable felt something strange in her chest and was rushed to a hospital in Santa Monica. They discovered she had lung cancer, and after a short tour of *Born Yesterday* in Florida, the actress returned to Los Angeles, where she died on July 3, 1973. According to one biographer, when daughter Jessica opened Grable's safety deposit box after the star's burial at Inglewood Park Cemetery near Los Angeles International Airport, it was empty except for a note that read, "Sorry, there's nothing more."

The life of another pinup girl was sadder. Petite (which made her the perfect costar for Alan Ladd, her equally diminutive Paramount colleague) and usually photographed with her face half obscured by a curtain of hair, Veronica Lake was, like Grable, a favorite of GI's during World War II. Whereas many careers have been finished because of lack of talent (Lake, though no thespian, was adequate in such films as 1942's *This Gun for Hire* and *I Married a Witch*), it was her looks—actually, her hairstyle, copied by thousands of women—that she claimed finished her in Hollywood, and it was all the fault of the First Lady, Eleanor Roosevelt. Seems that at one point in the early years of the war, Roosevelt suggested in her syndicated newspaper column, *My Day*, that since so many women working in the war industry were getting their Veronica Lake–styled hair caught in machinery, they should cut it short. The government then weighed in with the demand that Lake herself cut it short in 1943's *So Proudly We Hail*, in which she played an army nurse.

Since her career continued for nearly another decade after Mrs. Roosevelt's suggestion, it is far more likely that changing audience tastes had more to do with her decision to abandon Hollywood for theater following bankruptcy in the early 1950s. In 1962, syndicated gossip columnist Dorothy Kilgallen discovered her working as a hostess at a coffee shop in Manhattan's Murray Hill neighborhood. Then, after failed comeback attempts as a Baltimore television talk show hostess and costarring again with Ladd in the 1966 movie *Footsteps in the Snow*, she more or less gave up. Veronica Lake died of hepatitis while visiting friends in Vermont on July 7, 1973, four days after Betty Grable's death. Only thirty people attended her funeral; she was cremated and her ashes were scattered at sea.

Confronted with equally daunting challenges, another pinup girl *didn't* give up and was rewarded with a gratifying second career. Television may have named their 1993 homage to Jean Harlow *The Blonde Bombshell* (it starred Sharon Stone), but for most film fans the term will always be inseparable from the vivacious comedienne and singer named Betty Hutton, born Elizabeth June Thornburg in Battle Creek, Michigan, on February 26, 1921. By the age of three, Hutton was singing with her older sister, Marion, to entertain patrons swilling bathtub gin in the speakeasy their mother opened in their home to make ends meet after her husband deserted the family (Marion would go on to a career singing with the Glenn Miller Orchestra).

By fifteen she was singing with professional bands in Detroit, where the then famous radio bandleader Vincent Lopez heard her, signed her on the spot, and moved her to New York. In 1939, and known as "the blonde bombshell" for her sparkling personality, she appeared in a few musical shorts before being signed by producer

B. G. (Buddy) DaSylva to star on Broadway in *Panama Hattie*. When DaSylva became production chief of Paramount in 1941, he hired her to star in *The Fleet's In*; it was the beginning of a decade-long Hollywood career for Hutton, during which she made fourteen films including *Happy Go Lucky, Here Come the Waves* (with Bing Crosby), *The Perils of Pauline, Let's Dance* (with Fred Astaire), *Red, Hot, and Blue*, and her only straight dramatic role in a comedy film, *The Miracle of Morgan's Creek*. However, it was her sensational performance in the title role in the 1950 film based on Irving Berlin's hit musical *Annie Get Your Gun* (which Hutton got after Judy Garland was suspended for drug and alcohol problems) that established her as a major star. She followed this triumph with equally memorable performances in the same year's *Let's Dance* and 1952's *The Greatest Show on Earth* and *Somebody Loves Me* before contract problems with the studio resulted in her career coming to an abrupt halt. Although she made a brief appearance in the 1957 film *Spring Reunion*, trying to make ends meet with occasional club and television gigs simply wasn't enough and she declared bankruptcy in 1967, listing debts of $150,000. Things got worse; Hutton, like many other frustrated actors, began to find solace in drugs and alcohol, divorced her fourth husband (trumpeter Peter Candoli), fell out with her children, attempted suicide, and had a nervous breakdown.

Then fate in the person of Father Peter Maguire, a priest at St. Anthony's Parish in Portsmouth, Rhode Island, stepped in. With his help, Hutton regained her strength and began working as a rectory cook and housekeeper. When Betty told Maguire that she wished that she had gotten a better education and earned a degree, the priest helped her enroll at Salve Regina University, where, with credit for life experience, she quickly earned a bachelor's degree and, two years later, an MA. The school, impressed with her work, then awarded her an honorary Ph.D. and she went on to teach acting.

In 1985, Betty Hutton was presented with an Award of Achievement by the Musical Theater Society of Emerson College in Boston, an honor presently to individuals who have contributed with distinction to the field of musical theater. She shares this honor with a distinguished list that includes Anne Baxter, Ray Bolger, Victor Borge, Gregory Hines, Chita Rivera, Stephen Sondheim, and Ben Vereen. Today she lives quietly with friends in Palm Springs, California. Sometimes, good girls do finish first.

When the Beatles first came to America, they were asked whom they would most like to meet of all film and television celebrities. They instantly said "Jayne Mansfield." It wasn't long before the fabulous four hooked up with the sex bomb at Hollywood's Whiskey-a-Go-Go nightclub, where the platinum-blonde, spectacularly endowed actress reportedly asked John Lennon if his shag haircut was real; Lennon immediately pointed at her famous breasts and quipped, "Are those real?" The visit ended when the late George Harrison sloshed his glass of scotch at the drunken Mansfield, missed, and hit another sex bomb of the era, Mamie van Doren, squarely in the face.

Although Mansfield's celebrity would hardly be as enduring as that of the Beatles—she was widely laughed at by a certain element of the population—she and with the seven-years-older Marilyn Monroe were the most famous personifications of the women who parlayed the lusty, busty look that had become popular in the 1950s into personal celebrity and a box office bonanza for their studios. Unlike Monroe, Mansfield had her priorities right. "I'd worry about becoming famous first," she claimed in a 1954 ghostwritten biography, "then an actress."

Blinded by today's obsession with Monroe, many forget how

famous Mansfield was in the middle of the last century, her astonishing measurements celebrated in everything from an hourglass-shaped hot water bottle to the "boob-bumpers" of the late 1950s Cadillacs. In fact, in a 1999 *Playboy* rating of the One Hundred Sexiest Women of the Century, Mansfield ranked second only to Monroe, and the film version of *Will Success Spoil Rock Hunter?* (her first film for Fox) was one of 1957's twenty top grossing movies, just a fraction behind Monroe's *Bus Stop*. She also was a trouper; her *Success* costar, Tony Randall, claimed he preferred working with Mansfield over Monroe (with whom he later starred in *Let's Make Love*): "At least she tried to be a professional," he said, "and she had a sense of humor."

Despite her stated career priorities, some still suspect there might have been an actor trying to get past all that top-heavy flesh, but at the time her lusty-busty image and pouty manner (attributes shared, of course, with Monroe) overpowered any artistic considerations. But, with a reported IQ of 163, Mansfield figured out what it took to become a star right from the start, even if some of the early honors such as Miss Tomato, Miss Freeway, Miss Electric Switch, Miss 100% Pure Maple Syrup, and the clearly appropriate Miss Negligee and Miss Nylon Sweater were somewhat dubious (she did turn down Miss Roquefort Cheese).

Mansfield's first film was a bit part in Howard Hughes's *Underwater,* and as Hughes's star, the famously endowed Jane Russell, didn't show up for a press junket in Las Vegas, Mansfield, who had an unerring sense of how to mix crass with class, knew exactly what to do. While an audience of dozens of paparazzi watched, she deliberately fell in the hotel's pool, broke the strap of her skintight red swimming suit, and came up, as they say, "bouncing." The press had a field day; she was, as *Variety* said at the time, "worth her weight in cheesecake." The "splash" was widely reported, and within days she received dozens of film offers and started a bidding war between Hughes and Hal Wallis of Warner Brothers, which Jayne ended by signing with Wallis. (In a 1980 television biopic, Loni Anderson, playing Mansfield and wearing a white swimming suit, *accidentally* falls into the pool. There was nothing accidental about it.)

Her early films were flops (*Prehistoric Women, The Female Jungle, Illegal*), but after Warner Brothers dropped her contract, she began to hit her stride with 1955's *The Burglar* and *Pete Kelly's Blues* and 1957's *The Girl Can't Help It* and *Will Success Spoil Rock Hunter?* in which she reprised the role of the brassy Rita Marlow she had created on Broadway two years earlier to rave reviews.

Vera Jayne Palmer was born on April 19, 1933, in Bryn Mawr, Pennsylvania, to Herbert Palmer, a lawyer, and his wife, Vera. After her father's death when she was three, Jayne's mother remarried and the family moved to Dallas, Texas. According to Jayne, it was when she discovered fan magazines that she decided she wanted to become an actress. On May 6, 1950, after discovering that she was pregnant, the seventeen-year-old high school junior married "the most handsome boy in the school," Paul Mansfield; after the birth of their daughter, Jayne Marie Mansfield, Jayne joined him in Austin, where he was attending the University of Texas. She also took classes (bringing her baby with her, as the couple couldn't afford a babysitter) and worked at three jobs—as a receptionist, selling books door-to-door, and as a model. When Paul went off to ROTC training the next year, Jayne and baby moved to Los Angeles, where she took acting classes at UCLA and reached the finals of the 1951 Miss Southern California beauty contest. After Paul was drafted in 1952, Jayne returned to Dallas, entered Southern Methodist University, worked as a model, and made her local stage debut in a production of *Death of a Salesman*, where a Paramount scout saw her and invited her to come to Hollywood. Two years later she and her daughter did exactly that, heading west in their Buick; at the California state line she stopped, got out of the car, knelt, kissed the ground, and shouted: "I'm home!"

The first thing Mansfield did in Hollywood was to follow up on the Paramount bid; she called the studio and said to the operator: "I want to be an actress. I've won many beauty contests. What do I do?" Call it naïveté or call it chutzpah, it worked and Mansfield was offered a screen test to play, of all things, Joan of Arc (she later said that whoever the director was that saw the test told her she was a good actress but that her figure kept distracting him). A few days later she tested for the lead in Billy Wilder's *The Seven Year Itch*, but, of course, the part went to a far more established actress who soon would become Mansfield's friendly rival: Marilyn Monroe. But it was enough to convince her that her future lay in Los Angeles instead of Dallas and Paul, now returned from Korea. After a nasty divorce (Paul tried to get custody of their child by providing the court with copies of nude modeling photos Jayne had made in Dallas), she was free. Then Jayne got her first big TV role, Lux Theater's fall 1954 production of *The Angel Went AWOL,* and the tale of how she got the part was much ballyhooed at the time. It seems that after unsuccessfully waiting for an interview three days, she sent the producer a card with the simple notation "40-22-34" (pretty dramatic for a five-foot five-and-a-half-inch tall, 117-pound woman) and got the part in thirty seconds.

Fueling her fame was a relentless publicity campaign that, when she was appearing in *Will Success Spoil Rock Hunter?* the following October in New York, grew so intense that the *NY Daily News* actually banned the publication of any more of her pictures. And there were many to ban; about this time she began relentlessly making public appearances at openings from corner restaurants to malls to promote her show (and later, her films), sometimes taking payment in the form of merchandise (years later when her career was all but finished, she was paid for appearing at the opening of a meatpacking plant with 250 pounds of beef).

Beef, in fact, was very much on the menu when, while still in New York, Jayne attended Mae West's revue and noticed one of the legendary sex queen's muscle-men cast members, the twenty-eight-year-old, Budapest-born Mickey Hargitay, then the current (1955) Mr. Universe and billed by West as "the most perfectly built man in the world." Reportedly, during the show when Mansfield was asked what she would like for dinner, she pointed at Hargitay and replied: "the beefsteak on the end." After Hargitay accompanied Mansfield to Brooklyn the following day for her crowning as Blossom Queen, the notoriously possessive West called a press conference and publicly demanded Mickey explain it was all for publicity. (Friends say Mansfield was the only woman Mae West, basically a kind person, truly hated.)

Mansfield started 1958 with a bang, marrying Mickey Hargitay wearing a pink lace gown (he gave her a ten-carat pink diamond ring) and settling into a celebrated eight-bedroom, thirteen-bath Mediterranean-style mansion at 10100 Sunset Boulevard in the tony Holmby Hills neighborhood of Los Angeles, built in 1935 by the popular 1920s crooner Rudy Vallee. By the time Jayne finished decorating the place, it was an icon of 1950s kitsch. For one thing, like her wedding gown and ring, *everything* was pink—a color more popular at the time than before or since (those of a certain age may remember the era's ubiquitous pink-and-gray color combination, used from everything from men's suit ensembles to the 1958 Chevrolet). The couple's pink living room was lined with pink-dyed mink, the telephones were decorated with pink rhinestones, and she drove a pink Jaguar, a gift from MGM to try to lure Mansfield away from Fox; the studio also gave her a three-year supply of pink champagne in which the actress bathed in a heart-shaped pink bathtub twice a week. The couple's bed was surrounded by pink neon lights and surmounted by a heart-shaped canopy and flying cupids. She also drove a pink Cadillac Eldorado, a gift from Mickey after the birth of their first child, Miklos (Mickey Jr.), and was often photographed cavorting in the heart-shaped pool inscribed on the bottom with "I love you, Jaynie" in gold mosaic tiles. There was even a mini zoo with dozens of dogs and cats, an elephant, monkeys, and ocelots. Not surprisingly, the place was dubbed the Pink Palace.

It was too good to last, of course. Just before a highly successful December 1960 Las Vegas gig with Mickey (resulting in a now-cult record album *Jayne Mansfield Busts Up Las Vegas*), she and Mickey made *The Loves of Hercules* (she was pregnant with their second son, Zoltan, at the time) in Italy. Despite the success of the LP and the money Fox was making renting her out to other filmmakers, the studio soon dropped her contract, and her film career degenerated into low-budget European films.

Determined to regain her American career, she made a sort of soft-core exploitation film, *Promises, Promises*, and, after appearing in the not-quite-altogether as *Playboy*'s regular February Valentine Girl for six years, took it all off for the magazine in 1963. Fueled by *Playboy* publisher Hugh Hefner's arrest on obscenity charges, it became the biggest-selling issue in the magazine's history, but neither it nor the movie did much to resurrect Jayne's career. She decided to hit the nightclub circuit with a burlesque-cum-striptease act, and for a while it was highly successful, but after the birth of their daughter, Mariska, in 1964 (today a television star, she appears as Olivia Bronson on *Law & Order: SVU*),

Mickey and Jayne divorced. There were problems—her declining career, of course, and rumors that she had slept with President John Kennedy several times (as well as novelist Henry Miller, actor Richard Egan, and designer Oleg Cassini), and the further rumors that Mariska was really the daughter of an actor named Nelson Sardelli. She had also met a new man, Matt Cimber, director of a road show of *Gentlemen Prefer Blondes* starring Mansfield, and was becoming more and more alcohol-dependent. All together, it spelled the end of the six-year marriage.

She soon married Cimber (the couple had a son, Anthony, in 1965), but other than a sold-out engagement at the Latin Quarter in New York, her professional life continued downhill. In 1966 he directed her in *Single Room Furnished*; it and 1967's *Spree!* would be her last films, and the couple were soon divorced.

At 2:15 A.M. on the morning of June 29, 1967, Jayne, her forty-year-old boyfriend and lawyer Sam Brody, and Mariska, Zoltan, and Miklos were returning to their hotel after a show at the Stevens Supper Club near Biloxi, Mississippi (where Mansfield was filling in for Mamie van Doren), when Brody's 1966 Buick Electra plowed into the rear end of a truck parked alongside the highway. Brody and Mansfield, only thirty-four years old, were killed instantly. Mansfield's children, who were in the backseat of the car were only slightly injured. The rumor at the time was that she had been decapitated in the accident, but the coroner later said that other than a separation of the scalp and skull in one area of her head, the body was intact (the rumor apparently started when one reporter at the scene saw the blonde bouffant wig that had flown off her head in the collision and jumped to the wrong conclusion).

Although the story would be later denied by her publicist, after her death a very strange tale started circulating. It claimed that Mansfield had always been fascinated with the occult and that in

1966, after meeting Anton LaVey, founder of the Church of Satan, she joined the cult. Then, following an argument with Brody (who, friends claimed, abused Mansfield and, using thousands of dollars in unpaid legal bills, blackmailed her into staying with him), LaVey put a curse on the lawyer, saying he would "die within a year." In fact, shortly afterward, the couple was involved in a serious car crash in Los Angeles and Zoltan was severely mauled during a visit to Jungleland in Thousand Oaks, California; despite Brody's feelings, Jayne credited her son's recovery to a ritual performed by LaVey.

The Pink Palace was subsequently owned by Cass Elliot of the Mamas and the Papas and later by crooner Engelbert Humperdinck. All of them tried to erase the gaudy pink from the home's exterior, but in the beginning, the pink color bled through the primer paint. Hollywood being Hollywood, this was immediately attributed by the supernaturally inclined to Mansfield's ghostly presence instead of the intensity of the original paint's pigment. Visitors also claimed seeing a ghost of Mansfield lying by the pool, and Humperdinck once said he had seen the apparition of Mansfield descending the stairs. Be that as it may, the singer sold the mansion in 1997 to the present owners for just under $4 million; the present color is sort of purple. And Hargitay? He's retired, but his name is still vividly alive in Hollywood via Mickey Hargitay's Plants, a nursery near the intersection of La Brea Boulevard and Franklin Avenue owned by his son, Mickey Jr.

Jayne Mansfield was buried in the family plot in Pen Argyl, Pennsylvania. It would be difficult not to believe that, with Marilyn Monroe's death five years earlier, a seemingly happier and simpler era ended. Although many actresses were, perhaps tragically in the case of Mansfield, respected more for what they looked like than how they acted, it was at least a giddier time, and for that lost innocence it is clearly missed today.

There was, however, no innocence but a lot of good-natured fun lost with the 1980 death of a platinum-blonde bombshell who began a career before Harlow was born and outlasted them all, dying at the age of eighty-seven. By essentially poking fun at the world's obsession with sex, she became a legend in her own time as well as, in later years, the reigning queen of camp. Her name, of course, was Mae West.

Long before she trekked to Hollywood in 1932, West had already made a name for herself in New York by titillating, tantalizing, and shocking theater and vaudeville audiences with some of the naughtiest plays, burlesque routines, and sharpest one-liners in entertainment history; the 1926 play she wrote in which she played a prostitute with a heart that *wanted* gold was, shockingly for the time (only six years after women gained the right to vote), simply named *Sex*. It created a furor, outraged the critics (the *New York Daily Mirror* headlined "*Sex* . . . a monstrosity plucked from a garbage can, destined to sewer"), got her arrested, and, of course, made her a household word. Within months, she would add to her notoriety by writing and producing a "homosexual comedy-drama" named *The Drag*, a daring move at a time when few people even admitted the existence of homosexuals.

A generation later, she claimed, probably because of the antigay climate of the McCarthy era, that *The Drag* was written to alert the public to the dangers of homosexuality, but she later backed off and said the play was meant to be a path-breaking plea for sexual liberty that "glorified" the gay lifestyle. West, herself famously heterosexual with a taste for muscle men, nevertheless had many gay friends; among them was Cary Grant, whose career—one that would make him the best known male actor in the world—was launched when

West cast and traded taunts with him in 1933's *She Done Him Wrong*. The film version of her sensationally successful 1928 Broadway play *Diamond Lil*, *She Done Him Wrong* broke *The Birth of a Nation*'s return engagement record with more than six thousand callbacks in six months. West soon followed it with *I'm No Angel* (also costarring Grant); together, they made her the most famous (or infamous) woman in the country, celebrated in song (Cole Porter's "Anything Goes"), art (Diego Rivera's mistress, the artist Frida Kahlo, painted her), cartoons, WPA murals (in San Francisco's Coit Tower), and journalism (*Variety* called her "as hot an issue as Hitler").

For one thing, far more than her appearance, which was rather dumpy despite a forty-three-inch bust (honored by the name of the ubiquitous WWII life jacket, the Mae West), it was her mouth that made her famous—not its allure, which inspired Salvador Dali to design a red sofa shaped like her lips—but what she said with it. Mae West got away with dialogue that few, even in today's liberated era, would ever have the nerve to utter. How about "I'm the lady who works at Paramount all day and Fox all night"? Or, responding in a routine with a fellow who claimed his height was "six foot, seven inches," quipped: "Well let's forget about the six foot and talk about the seven inches."

And those are among the *less* famous quotes of the dozens that highlighted West's career and became an inseparable part of her legend. Still sounding as freshly minted as the day she said them, others include the slyly lascivious "It's better to be looked over than overlooked," "Is that a gun in your pocket or are you just glad to see me?" "It's not the men in my life, it's the life in my men," and "When I'm good, I'm very good, but when I'm bad, I'm better" (from *I'm No Angel*). When a character exclaims in *Night after Night* "Goodness! What beautiful diamonds!" West snaps back a line she later used as the title of her 1959 autobiography: "Goodness had nothing to do with it, dearie." Most famous of them all was her invitation to Cary Grant in *She Done Him Wrong*, always misquoted as: "Come up and see me sometime?" (The actual quote: "Why don't you come up sometime 'n see me? I'm home every evenin'.") The line was an instant addition to the common language and was used again by West in 1947 for the title of a comic spy play, *Come On Up*.

Mary Jane West was born in Brooklyn, August 17, 1893, the first of three children born to Matilda (Tillie, who West later idealized) and John Patrick West, a one-time boxer, bouncer in a Coney Island dance hall, and bodyguard for local racketeers. By the age of seven she was appearing in vaudeville, billed as the Baby Vamp. West married at seventeen, but it didn't last long and she remained single the rest of her life ("Marriage is a great institution," she later quipped, "it's fine if you want to live in an institution").

Today, with women filling corporate presidencies and senatorial seats, it's hard to realize how daring she once was; as Mae West would later admit, it wasn't just what she said, it was how she said it. With her trademarked raised hip and lowered eyebrow, she could purr otherwise inoffensive lines with the seductive power of a striptease; in fact, West's smoldering delivery of the line "Would you, honey, like to try this apple sometime?" during an Adam and Eve parody on the Edgar Bergen radio show in 1937 (Don Ameche was Adam) got her banned from radio for several *years*.

Will Hayes, Hollywood's appointed censor, was furious, but he could do little about it, since there was little obscene in the actual words she used. And since her films unquestionably helped Paramount avoid bankruptcy during the Depression, she had much of the industry itself on her side as she astutely reminded everyone when she said: "Virtue is its own reward, but has no sale at the box office." That became a self-fulfilling prophecy when, more than the endless drumbeat of complaints from the Hays office and her own increasingly cartoonlike persona—she was actually beginning to become a caricature of herself—it was her first box office failure that brought her down. *Klondike Annie*, the saga of an entertainer implicated in a murder who flees to Alaska and is transformed into a moral crusader, seemed to fit the bill for Paramount, which was pressuring West into tamer and tamer stories. Despite the censor's and studio's oversight, however, the film turned out not to be the redemptive story that got its script a 1935 Production Code seal of approval but the most controversial picture of her career, loaded with innuendo that seemed to glorify vice and outraged the religious community.

Although West made two more films for Paramount (1937's *Go West Young Man* and the following year's *Every Day's a Holiday*), the studio cancelled her contract. In 1939 Universal cast her in *My Little Chickadee,* a film, virtually free of any double entendres, through which West, who loathed the movie and her costar (W. C. Fields), seems to be sleepwalking.

In 1944, she wrote and starred on Broadway in a play about Catherine the Great, the Russian empress whom West considered "a warm, gay, very sensual woman, and yet a monarch who was a skillful politician . . . after my years of surviving studio politics, I saw Catherine was really a portrait of myself." The reviews were devastating, and she withdrew to her cream-colored, two-bedroom aerie in the Ravenswood apartments at 570 North Rossmore Avenue in Los Angeles to nurse her wounds. (Many people today believe she owned the building; she didn't, but rented her sixth-floor apartment there for forty-eight years.)

Six years later, Billy Wilder contacted her to star as Norma Desmond, the reclusive, once-famous star who attempts a comeback in what was originally a much lighter-themed *Sunset Boulevard*. West instantly rejected the offer, insulted that anyone would consider her a has-been, and toured the country for the next few years with a nightclub revue in which she was joined—to Jayne Mansfield's earlier-mentioned delight—by eight weightlifters clad only in loincloths.

In the early 1960s, a major Mae West revival began, revering her not as a sex-goddess but as the reigning monarch of a cultural phenomenon that celebrated the outrageous, the garish, and often the tasteless. Based on her one-liners (Decca even released an LP of them) and flamboyant reputation, and given the imprimatur of intellectualism by Susan Sontag in her widely excerpted essay, "Notes on Camp," Mae West became the "hip" queen of camp. "Camp is the kinda comedy where they imitate me," she quipped at the time.

Unfortunately, she had no idea of how to market her new persona, and the results were the disastrous films *Myra Breckenridge* (in which she played a lascivious Hollywood agent in the 1970 film version of Gore Vidal's novel) and *Sextette*, made in 1977, when she was eighty-four. After Rex Reed, a *Myra Breckenridge* costar, rather unchivalrously described her appearance in the latter film as "something they found in the basement of a pyramid," he tried to call to apologize, but West wouldn't talk to him.

On November 22, 1980, three weeks after returning home from a lengthy hospital stay following a stroke, Mae West died. Like many actors, she had a monumental ego, but she would often make fun of it, a saving grace that endeared her to her friends. She was also involved in spiritualism and was convinced that after her death—West was realistic in accepting the fact that she wouldn't last forever—she probably would continue vamping forever on another spiritual plane. One hopes she was right.

Mae West is buried in the family mausoleum in the gloomy Cypress Hills Cemetery in Brooklyn. It's hardly a final setting one would have expected for a star who, for so many years, added so much to glitter, the glamour, and sheer fun of Hollywood.

Much of modern movie music—including such familiar scores a[s] [t]hose heard in the *Star Wars* and *Raiders of the Lost Ark* series— [i]nspired by the film scores composed in the late 1930s and 1940s b[y] [a]n Austrian immigrant named Erich Wolfgang Korngold. From chil[d]hood he was considered a prodigy possessing a musical talent rivalin[g] [t]hat of Mozart, but when he died in 1957 he had long been dismisse[d]

Movies' Music

Despite the fact that most observers date the arrival of "sound" in Hollywood from 1927's *The Jazz Singer* (not entirely true, but close enough), sound—originally in the form of musical accompaniment—has always been part of the movie experience. It was *talking* that arrived in 1927, well recognized at the time when movies made with the new process were called talkies.

Sometimes it was only a tinkling piano that accompanied silent images, its music improvised by (or lifted from popular classical pieces) and fitted to the scene . . . marching music for parades, sad music for tragedy, giddy music for happiness, and so on. Later the music was provided by organs, once standard equipment in every respectable movie theater (or "movie palace," as the more sumptuous were beginning to be called); hence "the Mighty Wurlitzer" of yore, named for the showcase, huge instrument made by America's premier manufacturer of theater organs. Later, at least in the biggest theaters, full orchestras would supply music. But soon—at least after technology finally allowed moviemakers to actually print more than one soundtrack on the film (allowing them to drop the clearly unsatisfactory stopgap measure of having the movie's sound on synchronized phonograph records)—film sound as we know it would begin its evolution. Today, many credit a third to a half of a film's success to its music.

When the talkies arrived, they brought a huge physical as well as cultural disruption to the industry. Not only did Hollywood completely revise its way of making films ("Quiet on the soundstage!"), it also had to completely retool its equipment and replace the outdoor stages lit largely by nature with huge, artificially lit buildings that quickly came to be known as soundstages. In addition, thousands of theaters across the country had to be modified to show the new movies. Thousands of jobs were eliminated or lost because of the new technology, and not even the most famous actors were immune; the thick accents of the era's top stars quickly ended their careers, as did the actual voice of silent heartthrob John Gilbert, which recorded badly. On the other hand, thousands of new jobs were created, both for filmmakers who understood the new science as well as musicians who performed the scores and actors who sounded convincing, many of whom were imported from the New York stage.

But the biggest change was philosophical: Silent films, perhaps best epitomized by the works of Charlie Chaplin, were mime shows; talkies were theatrical performances. Chaplin, famously, but in the end futilely, fought the change, believing that only silent films with their mimed action could be a truly universal medium. In fact, before talkies arrived, he made dozens of movies (many, of course, short and quickly made one- and two-reelers); after 1927 it took eight years for him to make *Modern Times* (which contained sound in only one scene) and thereafter he completed only five more films. None of them, most people felt at the time, were up to the quality level of his early efforts, and comparing such classic Chaplin silents as *The Gold Rush* with his final film, *The Countess from Hong Kong*, they were certainly right. But that doesn't mean that he was entirely wrong, either. As they were unencumbered by dialogue, silents—the great ones, anyway—by demanding viewers' complete attention while also allowing them to more or less write their own scripts as the films unreeled, could be more subtle and carry a far greater impact than even today's blockbusters.

That also seems true today when, three-quarters of a century after they were written off as being hopelessly outdated as the horse and carriage (and many deliberately destroyed), movie buffs are flocking to silent film festivals in London, Italy, and San Francisco and to regularly scheduled showings across America. Many of them discovered the allure of silents via Turner Classic Movies' "Silent Sunday Night" screenings, and as Turner's huge inventory of silent movies includes a hundred or so films that have never been musically scored, the cable giant has also commissioned musicians to write new music for them.

In the heyday of the silent film, though, it was less important to write new music than to know what (and how) to steal. Although audiences may have been dancing the Black Bottom or the Charleston and listening to popular romantic ballads sung by popular crooners such as Rudy Vallee, when it came to movies, classical music—or bleeding chunks of familiar classical music—reigned. And despite today's erosion of the classical music market, to a surprising extent it still provides a vast inventory for movie scores. Especially popular is the thickly orchestrated, emotionally saturated music of the German composer Richard Strauss (no relation to Vienna's waltz king Johann Strauss Jr.) and Gustav Mahler, (born in Bohemia, later part of Czechoslovakia), whose heart-on-sleeve works are certainly among the most popular with classical music audiences these days.

That's not to say that all movie music, then or now, is derivative. Much of it is new, and much of it is memorable. But we always have to remember who the famous film composer Dimitri Tiomkin thanked when accepting his Oscar in 1955 for scoring *The High and the Mighty*: "Johannes Brahms, Johann Strauss, Richard Strauss, Richard Wagner, Beethoven, Schubert, Haydn, Mendelssohn, Rimsky-Korsakov . . ." He later said he would have added more had not the award show's host, Bob Hope, cut him short.

Then, of course, there are the two indispensable Russians: Pyotr Tchaikovsky and Sergei Rachmaninoff. Rachmaninoff in particular; his lushly romantic works have been a vein of pure gold mined by countless composers for film music (Frank Sinatra's 1946 hit song "Full Moon and Empty Arms" was lifted from the score of David Lean's romantic tearjerker of the same year, *Brief Encounter*, which was itself lifted from Rachmaninoff's Second Piano Concerto). "Rachh-maninoff?" Marilyn Monroe remarks to Tom Ewell in *The Seven-Year Itch*. "The Second Piano Concerto," he explains. "It isn't fair," she says. "Not fair? Why?" "Every time I hear it I go to pieces." So, in fact, do a lot of people.

So who was Sergei Rachmaninoff? Gaunt, tall, and aloof, he was certainly an unlikely candidate for film score immortality (albeit secondhand in most cases). Born the son of an alcoholic army officer near Novgorod, Russia, on April 1, 1873, Sergei was a problem child who failed at most of his classes but excelled at playing the piano. But four years at the Moscow Academy straightened him out and he graduated with honors and a commendation from Tchaikovsky. Nevertheless, the critics savaged his early works and it took three years of hypnotism to restore his creative confidence to the point he could begin his Second Piano Concerto in 1900. It was an instant hit, and nine years later, an adoring public received him on the first of many American tours with open arms. Following the Russian Revolution in 1917, he briefly settled in Stockholm but soon moved to New York, where he bought a house on Riverside Drive (and decorated it in a style that could only be described as "Czarist Imperial"). Before then he had written some 135 compositions; after his move to America there would be only ten more. But that was all it took to make him as popular—then and now— as his compatriot Tchaikovsky, Brahms, and other famous romantic composers.

In 1942, Rachmaninoff moved to Beverly Hills for his health but died only months later, on March 28, 1943, just a few weeks after attaining his American citizenship and only five days before his seventieth birthday.

The list of classical composers who have been a continuing resource for film scores could go on and on. It's Grieg's Piano Concerto that's being pounded out by the child molester when he is killed in the 1997 remake of *Lolita*, and 1993's *Shine* revolves around the story of a young man's effort to conquer Rachmaninoff's Third Piano Concerto (the composer's last public appearance was, in fact, at a Hollywood Bowl performance of this concerto by Vladimir Horowitz in the late summer of 1942). Occasionally, it works the other way around; so memorable was the use of the slow movement of Mozart's Piano Concerto no. 20 in an otherwise obscure 1967 Swedish film, many people since know the music only as the *Elvira Madigan Concerto*.

Actually, in the late 1930s and early 1940s, a vogue developed for classical concertos written expressly for movies, apparently inspired by the success of the 1938 film *Moonlight Sonata* that starred the legendary Polish pianist (and national hero) Ignace Jan Paderewski. The sheet music for Richard Addinsell's *Warsaw Concerto* from 1941's *Dangerous Moonlight* sold over 3 million copies in Britain and spawned some one hundred recordings of the pseudo-Rachmaninoff music. Later, the *Spellbound Concerto* derived from Miklos Rozsa's score for Hitchcock's 1945 Oscar-winning film of the same name became and remains extremely popular; less successful was Bernard Hermann's *Concerto Macabre* that accompanied the denouement of 1945's *Hangover Square* when a deranged pianist sets fire to a concert hall.

But the results don't always turn out as happily as *Elvira Madigan* or the *Warsaw Concerto*; there is probably no more hilariously inappropriate juxtaposition of music and action than the scene in Howard Hughes's 1943 film *The Outlaw* when Jane Russell and costar Jack Beutel tussle in a haystack to the accompaniment of Tchaikovsky's saccharine *Romeo and Juliet* suite. Nevertheless, marketed with unforgettable images of Russell's breasts that drove the Hollywood censor crazy, the film made the nineteen-year-old starlet famous. Part of the reason was the brassiere Hughes himself designed for Russell to wear in the film. Considering the fact that he also designed the retractable landing gear for airplanes for precisely the opposite need of streamling the curves, even if he wasn't too savvy about music, one has to admit Hughes was certainly multi-talented.

MGM's Irving Thalberg may have been the boy genius of film production, but, like Hughes, he was a bit of a blank page when it came to music. After hearing the lushly romantic *Verklarte Nacht* (Transfigured Night) composed by émigré Arnold Schoenberg long before he fled Europe for Hollywood in 1933, Thalberg called him into his office to invite him to compose the score for 1937's *The Good Earth*, based on Pearl Buck's novel about a Chinese peasant who becomes rich but loses his wife in the process. Thalberg told Schoenberg, then a five-thousand-a-year UCLA professor, that he wanted "oriental music." Schoenberg said he would write the music he wanted to and demanded total control of the film's sound, including dialogue that he planned to have the actors speak in the same pitch as his music. He also demanded fifty thousand dollars for the job that was, as he later explained, "fortunately, too much (money) for it would have been the end of me."

It seems clear that after generations have passed since composers began creating music for films, the most popular scores have been those that are the most romantic or dramatic. Hence the codependency on big-sound, big-emotion composers, which is understandable; like grand opera, movies depend to a great extent on big emotions, and they always have. Although he's a tremendously talented guy as acknowledged by five Oscars, there's a lot of similarity in style if not in actual tunes between John Williams (*Jaws, Star Wars, Saving Private Ryan*) as well as James Horner (*Titanic*) and the music of a number of famous opera composers. And don't think, like some classical music purists, that there is anything lowbrow about it all (many still look down their noses at Rachmaninoff's music despite its box office popularity). When, in 1988, he was asked what music he listened to most, Pope John Paul II told an interviewer that it was not something by Beethoven, Bach, or Mozart, as might be expected, but quintuple Oscar winner John Barry's score for *Dances with Wolves* (Barry also wrote the scores for the early James Bond films and won Oscars for *Out of Africa*, *Born Free*, and *The Lion in Winter*).

The public also loved the movie music of Alfred Newman, who, during a career ending with his death in 1970, chalked up dozens of Oscar nominations and won nine; among them 1938's *Alexander's Ragtime Band*, 1940's *Tin Pan Alley*, 1943's *Song of*

Bernadette, With a Song in My Heart (1951), and *Love Is a Many-Splendored Thing* in 1955. He also wrote Twentieth Century Fox's familiar fanfare. Like Johann Sebastian Bach, Newman also seemed to have started a family business—two of his children, David and Thomas, and his nephew, Randy, have also followed his career with great success. And Newman was only one of a half dozen composers who, a couple generations ago, were as famous as many of the biggest stars.

New York–born (1911) Bernard Herrmann began his march to film score fame writing music for radio dramas including Orson Welles's Mercury Theater of the Air (the selfsame company that scared the bejeezus out of America in 1938 with its realistic adaptation of H. G. Wells's *The War of the Worlds*), so when Welles came west to film *Citizen Kane* two years later, it was only natural that Herrmann would follow. *Kane*, considered by many as the greatest film ever made, is certainly the best Herrmann ever scored. Although he went on to provide the music for such successful films as *Jane Eyre, North by Northwest*, and *Vertigo*, nothing, in the opinion of many, came quite up to the level of *Citizen Kane* . . . except, of course, his music for Hitchcock's *Psycho*, especially his music for the terrifying shower scene.

Franz Waxman, born in Poland in 1906, gained his first fame for composing the brooding score for James Whale's 1931 *Frankenstein*. He won two more Academy Awards for *Sunset Boulevard* (1950) and *A Place in the Sun* the following year, drawing much of his inspiration from the music of Richard Wagner and, like many of his colleagues, Richard Strauss. And let us not forget one of America's most celebrated classical composers, Aaron Copland. Besides composing the scores for such ballets as *Billy the Kid* and *Appalachian Spring*, he wrote scores for nine films (among them *Of Mice and Men* and *Our Town*), winning an Oscar for 1949's *The Heiress*.

But it would be Dimitri Tiomkin, born in the Ukraine in 1899 and taught by Russian composers Alexander Glazanov and Dimitri Shostakovich, who would, despite his acknowledged indebtedness to several European classical composers, most memorably express the American spirit—its frontier spirit, anyway—in film music.

After living for a time in St. Petersburg, where he supported himself playing the piano for silent films, Tiomkin moved on to Berlin to live with his father, an assistant to Dr. Paul Ehrlich, the discoverer of "the magic bullet" that cured syphilis. There he studied with the composer Ferruccio Busoni and made his performing debut with the Berlin Philharmonic as a pianist. In 1925, he was invited to come to America as, of all things, half of a two-man vaudeville piano team for which he and his partner would receive the equally astonishing salary of a thousand dollars weekly.

In New York he soon met an married a ballerina named Albertina Rasch, returned to Europe briefly to premiere George Gershwin's Concerto in F in Paris, and, in 1930, moved with his wife to Hollywood, where MGM had commissioned her to create short film ballets to attract Depression-impacted audiences back into the theaters. After they arrived, Albertina talked up her husband's talents to anyone who would listen, and after a few false starts, Columbia's Frank Capra gave Dimitri his big break when he picked him to score *Lost Horizon* in 1936. A decade later, after being asked to write "some orgasm music" for *Duel in the Sun*, Tiomkin got involved, somewhat famously, in a duel of his own with the film's producer, David O. Selznick. When nothing the composer produced pleased Selznick, he famously complained: "It isn't orgasm music. It's not *shtump*; it's not the way I fuck." Tiomkin, undaunted, replied, "Mr. Selznick, you fuck your way, I'll fuck my way. To me, *that* is fucking music." Clearly the pair resolved their differences about relationship music and Tiomkin finished the score.

So what does this have to do with the American frontier spirit? In the ensuing years Tiomkin would score many classic Westerns such as *Giant* (1956), *Gunfight at the O.K. Corral* (1957), and *The Alamo* in 1960, but it was as the composer of 1952's *High Noon* that he would write one of the country's (and country music's) cultural classics, the famous ballad sung by Tex Ritter in the film: "Do Not Forsake Me, Oh My Darlin'." For both the film score and the song he won Oscars, and he would go on to win two more: for 1954's *The High and the Mighty* and *The Old Man and the Sea* four years later.

But, more so than anyone else, it would be the music of a thirty-seven-year-old émigré, in his youth considered as remarkable a prodigy as Wolfgang Amadeus Mozart, that bound together many of the most famous films of a half century ago. His trademarks, huge, noisy cues, propulsive adventure themes that seemingly employed every brass instrument ever invented, and melting, emotionally wrought melodies accompanying romantic scenes also became the stock-in-trade of just about every film composer since.

Gustav Mahler was among the first major composers to publicly recognize the talent of Erich Wolfgang Korngold, born in Brno, Czechoslovakia, in 1897; after meeting him when he was only ten, Mahler hailed the young composer as simply "a genius . . . a genius." Four years later, after hearing an overture composed by Korngold in 1911, Richard Strauss, composer of the popular opera *Der Rosenkavalier* (The Knight of the Rose) and programmatic tone poems such as *Don Quixote* and *Also Spracht Zarathustra* (used to telling effect in the opening scene of Stanley Kubrick's *2001*), wrote the youth's father, a prominent Viennese music critic: "Such mastery fills me with awe and fear." Giacomo Puccini, whose popular operas including *La Boheme* and *Tosca* have also been mined for movie music, agreed: "[Korngold] has so much talent," he wrote, "he could easily give us half and still have enough left for himself."

At eleven, Korngold composed an instantly popular ballet score that was given its premiere in a command performance for Emperor Franz Josef at the Vienna Court Opera. Six years later, his first two operas premiered as a double bill in Munich, cast with several of the greatest singers of the era and conducted by the later legendary Bruno Walter (later a Los Angeles neighbor). During the First World War he was appointed musical director of his regiment, which allowed him to continue composing through the war. It was during this period that Korngold began working on what would become his most successful (and enduring) opera, 1920's *Die Tote Stadt* (The Dead City). As the opera is about a man who believes his dead wife has been reincarnated as a ballet dancer, it's clear that Korngold was—at least subconsciously—already prepared for his later success in Hollywood.

In 1934 he arrived in America's film capital at the invitation of the impresario and director Max Reinhardt, specifically to arrange Felix Mendelssohn's *Midsummer Night's Dream* music for what would become a landmark production of Shakespeare's play at the Hollywood Bowl. He followed this with arranging the music for a subsequent film derived from the production, and within a year, Warner Brothers invited him to write an original score for *Captain Blood* starring Errol Flynn. Erich Korngold's second career had begun.

Korngold, who described his film music as "operas without singing," went on to write eighteen full-length feature film scores over the next twelve years. Among them were *Anthony Adverse* (for which he received the first of a pair of Oscars, actually awarded to the head of Warner's music department, Leo Farbstien, as was the policy of the time, in 1936); *The Adventures of Robin Hood* (his second Oscar, awarded in 1938. On the day he signed the contract to compose the music, Hitler's puppet government in Austria banned his music, effectively exiling him from his homeland); other scores included *The Private Lives of Elizabeth and Essex* (1939); *King's Row* (1942); and *Of Human Bondage* (1946).

In 1949, Korngold returned to Vienna in the hopes of resuming his career, but his by then old-fashioned neo-Romantic style was received with disinterest or savage criticism, especially his fifth and last opera, *Die Kathrin*, which, after the Nazi ban, was finally premiered in Vienna in 1950. Disheartened by the experience, he returned to Hollywood, made concessions to the modern style of composition with his Symphony in F-sharp, a cello concerto, several string quartets, and a violin concerto (commissioned and premiered by Jascha Heifetz), and made plans for a sixth opera. Unfortunately, Korngold became ill before it got under way, and he died of a cerebral hemorrhage on November 29, 1957, at the age of sixty. Following his death, the Vienna Opera House flew a black flag of mourning at half-mast. When she was told of the gesture, his widow commented, "It's a little late."

But it's never too late to be rediscovered. In an article on Korngold, the musicologist Nicolas Slonimsky wrote not long ago: "Ironically, his film scores, in the form of orchestrated suites, experienced long after his death a spontaneous renaissance, particularly on records, and especially among the unprejudiced and unopinionated American musical youth, who found in Korngold's music the stuff of their own new dreams."

Despite his later disappointment, Korngold was apparently more relaxed about his own dreams. Sometime before leaving Hollywood for his return to Vienna, he encountered fellow Viennese composer Max Steiner at Warner Brothers. "Tell me something, Korngold," Steiner—who composed, conducted, and orchestrated over three hundred film scores between 1928 and 1965 (among them *The Wizard of Oz*) and won three Oscars—asked. "We've both been at Warner's for ten years now, and in that time your music has gotten progressively worse and worse and mine has been getting better and better. Why do you suppose that is?" Without missing a beat, Korngold replied in his thick accent: "I tell you vy dat iss, Steiner. Dat iss because you are stealing from me and I am stealing from you."

Crosby, then at the height of his immense fame (a poll in the late 1940s showed him more popular than General Eisenhower), takes a proud lap (with, of course, his signature pipe) of the new Del Mar racetrack which he and several partners, including Pat O'Brien, Oliver Hardy, and Gary Cooper, owned on the opening, July 4, 1937, weekend.

Heigh-ho Hollywood

If there is one common denominator shared by the stars of the golden age of film, it is that most of them shared a passion for horses. Robert Wagner, one of the few still active stars whose career reaches back to the golden era of Hollywood, and a man who, with his wife, Jill St. John, owns a string of quarter horses, explains the attraction with the familiar quote: "Nothing is better for the inside of a man than the outside of a horse." (Wagner, all of whose friends call him R. J., made his debut in a bit part in 1950's *The Happy Years* with a baseball catcher's mask covering what would become one of the world's most famous faces; it was his performance as a wounded GI in *With a Song in My Heart*, 1952's biopic of singer Jane Froman, played by Susan Hayward, that made him a household name.)

But there is more to it than the spiritual relationship

between man and his form of transportation that endured for many more thousands of years than has the automobile. True, they were important for transportation in Hollywood's early days as well as everywhere else in the world (Cecil B. DeMille rode horseback between his home up the canyon where the Hollywood Freeway now runs, and his Hollywood studio). And although no one has directly linked the attraction, it seems clear that Hollywood's affinity for horses was also related to the basic insecurity of filmmakers, which caused them to adopt many European status symbols (particularly British), as well as the occasional title of prince or earl or countess, as part of their California lifestyle. Fake counts, countesses, earls, and princes, in fact, were all over the place, more common than the real thing attracted by the glamour (and money) of the film capital.

Also popular were English-style homes and English pubs imported for private bars, but especially popular was that very European, very aristocratic sport—polo. Polo required more free time than most busy actors had (like Will Rogers, Darryl Zanuck was a passionate advocate of the sport, but he was, of course, a boss).

By the 1930s, it must have seemed that everyone in Hollywood was riding a horse; in fact, the now lushly landscaped median strips on Sunset Boulevard in front of the Beverly Hills Hotel as well as that down the residential section of Beverly Hills' elegant Rodeo Drive were once bridal trails. Many of the golden age stars also owned horse ranches; most of them—because of the wide-open spaces that were undeveloped—were in the west end of the San Fernando Valley. Now, towns like Reseda, Granada Hills, and Northridge have overtaken even the smallest piece of open space, and countless ancient California sycamore and eucalyptus trees that used to perfume the air have been uprooted to make way for mini-malls, fast-food restaurants, and shopping centers. But once upon a time (not so long ago), one could see little else but empty meadows tied together by seemingly endless ribbons of white fencing.

One of the pioneers to ranch the San Fernando Valley was author Edgar Rice Burroughs, whose most famous literary creation was, of course, Tarzan. He bought his 540-acre spread, originally chosen by the *Los Angeles Times* publisher, General Harrison Gray Otis, as a site for a future home, in 1919. He named it Tarzana and raised goats and chickens on the spread, adding riding stables and horses for his children within a few years. Burroughs later subdivided the ranch, and the name was adopted for the thriving community that later grew up on the site in 1927. The adobe-style house that served as his office can still be found tucked away in a grove of eucalyptus trees alongside busy Ventura Boulevard, and it was there that Burroughs's ashes (he died in 1950) were stored in a desk drawer for more than a decade before being strewn over the vacant lot on nearby Reseda Boulevard, later paved over to serve as the parking lot of Gelson's Market.

Barbara Stanwyck, a fine horsewoman, owned a three-hundred-acre spread with Zeppo Marx a bit to the west of Tarzana named Mar-Wyck. Not far away was Robert Taylor's smaller spread, one of two horse ranches he owned in Los Angeles (Taylor and Stanwyck were married from 1939 to 1951). Fred Astaire owned a ranch nearby; so did the once famous radio hillbilly comedy team of Lum and Abner (Chester Lauck and Norris Goff). Farther up the road in Moorpark, Charles K. Howard and Bing Crosby owned a ranch, originally called Ridgewood but later Melodyland, where Howard's legendary racehorse Seabiscuit (who in 1937, it is claimed, garnered more headlines than Roosevelt, Hitler, and Mussolini combined) was buried when he died in 1947; Robert Wagner owned the place in the early 1990s and notes that even then, fourteen years after Crosby's death, the airplane hangar and landing strip he built at the ranch remained intact.

Howard was a partner in the Santa Anita racetrack built in 1933, and he was also a partner with Crosby in the mission-style racetrack the crooner built by the Pacific Ocean in 1936 close by his sixty-five-acre ranch on the old Don Juan Osuna land grant just north of San Diego. The track, now one of the most popular in America, was the sun around which most of the horse-loving movie stars revolved for years; so passionate was Crosby about the project that when he and his associates (who included actors Pat O'Brien, Oliver Hardy, and Gary Cooper) ran out of money during construction, Crosby (and O'Brien) borrowed a combined six hundred thousand dollars from their life insurance policies to finish it. Its name is Del Mar, and it opened before a star-packed audience of fifteen thousand on July 3, 1937 (appropriately, Bing's horse, High Strike, won the first race).

As one writer has said: "Del Mar still evokes the relaxed, easygoing feeling of what horse racing used to be before the advent of the tote board and the discovery by politicians that there was money to be made from it . . . where nobody is in a hurry but the horses." Built with the partial financing from Franklin Roosevelt's Works Projects Administration, a program designed to put people to work during the Depression years, the grandstands were actually built of adobe bricks, made from mud dug on the site. A decade ago, the track was completely rebuilt in a similar mission-style architecture (no more adobe, though!) under the stewardship of the Del Mar Thoroughbred Club's president and CEO, Joe Harper—appropriately, the grandson of Cecil B. DeMille.

In its heyday, a special train from Los Angeles served the track, but the parties often became so rowdy (like that following the world premiere of Crosby's 1938 musical *Sing, You Sinners*, which was projected on a special screen facing the stands) that many people missed the last train at 2:00 A.M.

Both Bob Hope and Crosby claimed that Hope's impromptu appearances with Bing entertaining at press parties in the late 1930s inspired them to collaborate professionally on their celebrated series of *Road* pictures, which began with 1940's *Road to Singapore* (other entertainers included Al Jolson, Danny Thomas, Tony Martin, and Donald O'Connor). Mickey Rooney piloted his own plane from Santa Monica to Del Mar's airport almost daily in the summer of 1940. By then, another show business legend, Jimmy Durante, was spending his summers at the track; he died in 1980, but his widow, Marge, is still often seen during Del Mar's seven-week racing season, which for more than a decade has topped the nation in daily attendance.

By 1937, Crosby's show, the *Kraft Music Hall*, was the number-one radio program in the nation, so it probably wasn't too much of a problem for him to convince sponsors and NBC to put on a radio show every Saturday morning from the track. The next year, Crosby introduced a song he cowrote to a tune composed by James Monaco that is still played before the first and after the last race of every day's program; it's said that to people around the track, it's as well known as the national anthem:

There's a smile on every face
And a winner in each race
Where the turf meets the surf at Del Mar.

Much of this came to an end on December 7, 1941, and during the war, wing ribs for the B-17 Flying Fortresses were manufactured on assembly lines set up in the grandstand. A year after hostilities ended, Crosby, C. K. Howard, and O'Brien sold their stock and the new owners brought in Mike Todd; his first and hardly well thought out move was to give away free copies of a book containing several of Damon Runyon's short stories about the track, entitled *All Horse Players Die Broke*, to all of the track's patrons on opening day.

Still, the glamour of Hollywood remained and to a great extent still does. Harry James and his wife, Betty Grable, were a fixture in the 1940s; one of their colts was named after James's famous trumpet, Big Noise. The FBI's now infamous boss, J. Edgar Hoover, was a summer regular (he was a two-dollar bettor who used his annual physical checkups at the nearby Scripps Institute as an excuse for hanging around the track in the afternoons), as were Lucille Ball and Desi Arnaz. They often raced their own horses; after the couple divorced in 1960, Arnaz retired to a home on the beach near the track, where he died in 1986.

But you don't have to go as far as Del Mar to still find traces of what it was like in Hollywood when the horse was, after studio management, of course, king. From the rustic stables at the West Los Angeles home shared by Robert Wagner and his wife, Jill St. John, the couple can and often do ride their favorite horses through the Santa Monica Mountains to the Pacific Ocean. "It's like it used to be in Hollywood before air-conditioning," Wagner recently reminisced, "you can still smell the orange blossoms." And not once along their nine-mile route through one of the most popular residential areas of the second largest city in America do they have to cross a single road or highway. It's another part of Hollywood that isn't entirely lost.

Paul R. Williams was the first African American anywhere to become
a prominent architect. He designed homes for stars from Lucille Ball
to Frank Sinatra, and was also a member of many civic organizations.
In his role as president of Los Angeles's Municipal Art Commission,
he and Anthony Quinn view Vincent van Gogh's painting *L'Arlesi-
enne,* part of a local exhibit, in a photograph taken in 1957.

The Stars Build Their Dream Homes

Because of the climate and the vast spaces available for living, working, and playing, Los Angeles was committed to the automobile from the beginning of the motor age. In fact, in 1934, at the intersection of Pico and Westwood Boulevards in West Los Angeles where today the huge Westside Pavilion houses dozens of shops and restaurants in postmodern splendor, an entrepreneur named Ralph M. Hollingshead opened the second drive-in theater in America. (The first, also built by Hollingshead, who had actually received a patent for the innovation, was in Camden, New Jersey).

As the twentieth century sped up thanks to more powerful cars and especially the evolving importance of the airplane, so did the influence of streamlining on the design of everything from toasters and vacuum cleaners to radios and, of course, cars themselves. The roads those faster cars drove on had to improve, too, and the first freeway built in the West was Los Angeles's 8.2-mile, downtown-to-Pasadena Arroyo Seco Freeway, started in 1938 and later renamed for its destination.

Inevitably, the movement, called Streamline Moderne, also forced architects to begin discarding the city's entrenched Spanish Revival look and rethink what they were doing. And nowhere else in America did the streamlined look find richer soil to grow in than in Hollywood and Los Angeles. In the 1930s, alongside zigzaggy Art Deco temples such as the Bullocks Wilshire department store and the glorious Spanish Revival Union Station (built in 1938), many residences, and commercial and public buildings including 1935's much missed Pan-Pacific Auditorium, began to sport voluptuous curves and even speed lines to presumably convey the impression that the entire edifice and its visitors were speeding down some highway to the future.

The automobile also changed the very orientation of many buildings and established a pattern familiar today; the entrance to Bullocks Wilshire, for example, as well as to nightclubs such as Hollywood's Palladium Ballroom, the nearby Earl Carroll Theater (now the headquarters of Nickleodeon), and the Hotel Roosevelt face not the street but their parking lots. There were other innovations created by the car, too; the most obvious was the birth of uses for the drive-in other than movies.

While not all of the drive-in innovations were unique to Los Angeles, there is no question that many were perfected there; some, which were to become stereotypical of the American lifestyle in later years, actually were born in the City of the Angels. The first drive-in bank in America was the Security-First National Bank built in 1937 in Vernon, a suburb of Los Angeles. Even more significant in the great scheme of things, the drive-in restaurant probably first appeared in Hollywood when, in 1929, Carpenter's

Drive-in opened on Sunset Boulevard. Motels arrived, not originally built for travelers traveling from one place to another but as small, automobile-oriented urban hotels; no place had more of them per capita than Hollywood.

Always on the lookout for something new, the film industry wasted little time jumping on board the Moderne Streamliner, evangelizing the new look ceaselessly in such films as those churned out by Busby Berkeley and the Astaire/Rogers dance romances of the 1930s; by 1935, thanks in large part to Hollywood's influence, the streamlined look had become the *in* style in communities across America.

Fantasy has always been a part of architecture, since the Hanging Gardens of Babylon were supposedly created by Nebuchadnezzar II six hundred years before the birth of Christ, and it has played a significant part in the architecture found in Los Angeles from its earliest years. Although he'd certainly deny it, fantasy's most famous exponent in the silent era of films was probably Frank Lloyd Wright, who designed five houses showcasing his intricately patterned "textile-block" construction in eccentrically escapist styles. Among them was the Inca-influenced Hollyhock House, built in Hollywood in 1919 for a philanthropist named Aileen Barnsdall, and the huge Mayan-temple-that-never-was-built a decade later for a haberdasher named Charles Ennis on a high hill, also in Hollywood (it has been seen by millions in numerous movies, including 1991's *The Rocketeer*). As with many of Wright's houses, the engineering of these homes came nowhere near matching the brilliance of the concept—on most rainy days, area residents are used to seeing the architecture of such treasures partially covered with bright blue tarpaulins, as all share a common Wrightsian attribute: leaky roofs.

In the 1930s, fantasy as programmatic architecture also ran

rampant, from the Darkroom, a small Wilshire Avenue camera store designed to resemble a camera (now a restaurant), to the gigantic tire plant on Central Avenue near downtown Los Angeles designed to look like a Babylonian temple. There was and still are dozens of other examples in the city, including the much mourned Brown Derby Restaurant on Wilshire Boulevard, designed as a derby hat (its crown, removed and painted puce, now ignominiously tops an Asian restaurant in a strip mall); the Tail of the Pup hot dog stand, designed to look like a hot dog, in Beverly Hills; Hollywood's 1936 Crossroads of the World office complex, surrounding a main building designed by Robert V. Derrah to look like a boat (albeit tugboat sized), complete with portholes and a turning globe, representing the world, atop a tower. But that's nothing compared to Derrah's Coca-Cola bottling plant, which looks like a concrete ocean liner landlocked on Central Avenue in Los Angeles. Designed in 1937, it is complete with a flying bridge, portholes, and deck railings. There was more than surface appeal to this building as well. At the time, the ocean liner was equated with the machine and with cleanliness, and thus, as pointed out in David Gebhard and Harriette von Breton's book *Los Angeles in the Thirties*, the building also could subconsciously be equated with the conveyor-belt production of the soft drink as well as the hygienic nature of a bottling plant. Of course, the modern streamlining was more obviously symbolic of the up-to-date nature of Coca-Cola.

Many people today don't realize there was a long history of programmatic architecture in Los Angeles. In 1926, long before anyone ever thought of a coffee stand designed to resemble a doughnut, a society matron named Christine Sterling, with the financial support and political clout of Harry Chandler, publisher of the *Los Angeles Times*, built one of the country's first theme parks when she created the quaint Olvera Street development as a nostalgic but fictitious trip back to the city's Spanish origins.

She wasn't done, though. Seven years later, and again with Chandler's support, Sterling headed up the rebuilding of the city's Chinatown as a sort of kitsch Asian Disneyland, where torii gates, theme restaurants, and lots of red and gold dragons sadly, as far as old-timers were concerned, replaced the earlier brothels and casinos. And speaking of never-never lands: Few remember anymore that despite the community's salubrious climate, Westwood Village (next to the UCLA campus) boasted a tourist theme park attraction in 1939 called the Tropical Ice Gardens, incongruously decorated with cutouts of northern pine trees set among tile-roofed Spanish buildings. Could all of this have been the dormant inspiration for Walt Disney when he first thought of creating a family theme park adjacent to his Burbank studio two years later? (Construction of the original park was put on hold by World War II; ground was broken for the much larger Disneyland, located on a 180-acre citrus grove in Anaheim, in 1954.)

Not everyone was convinced by the new Streamline look, though, and most architects were not at all interested in programmatic or theme architecture. R. M. Schindler and Richard Neutra, both European émigrés, were only the most outstanding of many architects who chose to stick to the modern (as opposed to the trendy Moderne) International Style, defined by a glass-shrouded, functional look and espoused by such leaders as the legendary Mies van der Rohe (who, tellingly, seems never to have been approached to design a building in Hollywood). Like much of the high-end furniture of the era designed by van der Rohe and, later, Eero Saarinen and others, the culturally challenging International Style was largely for connoisseurs. Aside from some showcase apartments (including the stunning Strathmore apartment complex near UCLA designed by Neutra in 1937), homes (among them Neutra's astonishing 1936 exercise in curvilinear architecture for director Josef von Sternberg's long since razed Northridge home), and commercial buildings including CBS's still-used Hollywood studios (designed by William Lescaze and E.T. Heitschmidt in 1936)—the film capital wasn't particularly interested in the look.

In fact, if there is a defining theme to the taste of Hollywood power elite, it is that they most often always chose "feel-good" architecture for their offices and homes, erecting buildings that either reminded them of home or comfortable classic styles like that of Mount Vernon, which was evoked by Goldwyn Studio's headquarters. And it's still true: Steven Spielberg's headquarters on the Universal Studio lot is nothing less than a re-creation of a cozy Santa Fe adobe.

Aside from a few examples, such as the famous Jack and Jill house in Beverly Hills that looks like something from a book of fairy tales, stars have been far more conservative in the choice of their own personal dwellings than the cutting-edge designs that they frequently inhabited in their movies. Errol Flynn's Mulholland Farm, for example, which probably masked more sexual carryings-on than any other house in Hollywood, looked like a fairly ordinary Cape Cod cottage. Although younger stars such as *ER*'s Noah Wylie and Madonna have sought out Spanish Revival homes built in Hollywood during the 1920s and 1930s, Robert Wagner, who moved out of his colonial home in Beverly Hills after his wife Natalie Wood's death in 1981, chose a splendid example of the spread-out ranch house designed by Cliff May in 1936, a dozen miles west of Hollywood. In fact, as popular as the movie and Moderne architecture was at the time, it was not in Hollywood but in Denver, Colorado, that a scaled-down copy of the famous Streamline-styled lamasery designed for 1937's *Lost Horizon* was built (by one of the major stockholders in Columbia, the studio that made the movie).

So it's somewhat ironic that a famed architect who, from the 1920s until his death in 1980, gave the stars exactly what they wanted—home designs with enough of an element of modernity to make them semi-hip—is largely forgotten today. Making his relative obscurity even odder is the fact that, in 1962, in association with two other architectural firms, he designed what would become perhaps Los Angeles' most familiar landmark, the futuristically arched Theme Building at LAX. Perhaps it is because what he designed was so safe: commercial buildings like the now shuttered Perino's Restaurant, a favorite of Hancock Park society that generally eschewed film people, and Beverly Hills's Chasen's, a favorite of celebrities (now a supermarket) that restricted gimmickry to such publicity-producing innovations as their famous flaming martini and an eater-friendly chili, so popular that it was often flown to Rome for Elizabeth Taylor during the filming of *Cleopatra*.

It is particularly ironic that the same architect who would one day design homes for Frank Sinatra, Lucille Ball and Desi Arnaz, Tyrone Power, and Lon Chaney would not have been welcome in any of the neighborhoods where they were built—certainly not in Hancock Park before Nat King Cole and his wife, Maria, broke the unwritten color barrier when they moved in—because Paul Revere Williams, designer of more than three thousand buildings that included offices for the film establishment, homes for many of the most famous stars of the era, schools, commercial buildings (including Saks Fifth Avenue and W. & J. Sloan), and churches hosting thousands, was one of the few successful architects in America who was black. He was, in fact, the first of his race to become a member (later, fellow) of the American Institute of Architects.

Paul Williams was born in Los Angeles on February 18, 1894, where his father, previously a waiter at the Peabody Hotel in Memphis, Tennessee, ran a fruit stand near Olvera Street, the historic origin of the city. Orphaned at four by the death of his parents, Paul was raised by a foster mother, picking up German (from new immigrants) and Chinese (from the laundry man in nearby Chinatown) in the increasingly polyglot city. He was the only "Negro" in his grammar school where he also became known as the class artist for the quality of his drawings, an interest that continued at the Polytechnic High School, where he took a class in architecture. Reflecting the general opinion of the era, when he told his instructor he wanted to be an architect, the man laughed and, as Williams often recalled, said, "Who ever heard of a Negro being an architect?" explaining that since blacks built neither fine homes nor office buildings, he would be entirely dependent on whites for his livelihood.

Williams, who later remembered this moment as the turning point in his life, decided to go ahead with his dream. After all, he thought, if he let the fact that he was black change his goal, he would always be defeated, and any prejudice on the part of white Americans would only be overcome through efforts on the part of black people to overcome cultural differences. It may have been naive, and it never would have worked in Atlanta or Little Rock at the time, but in Los Angeles, it was his key to success.

In 1914, at the age of twenty, Williams won a two-hundred-dollar first prize for a neighborhood civic center in Pasadena, and buoyed by other awards, he signed up for an architectural engineering course at USC and started looking for a job with an architectural firm. Out of dozens of interviews, he received three offers for work only as an office boy; two offering three dollars a week, the third, nothing. He chose the one paying nothing because it was with one of the best firms in the city, and he figured the experience would be invaluable. Williams figured correctly and swiftly moved up to paying jobs with that and other firms, learning everything he could from landscape and small-home design to engineering theaters when he assisted with the construction designs for the city's gigantic, five-thousand-seat Shrine Auditorium.

In 1922, Williams opened his first office with a ninety-thousand-dollar commission from a former employer; buoyed by the city's boom, within a decade he was designing hundreds of private and commercial buildings, among them E. L. Cord's thirty-two-thousand-square-foot Beverly Hills mansion named Cord-haven. Williams got the job by delivering sketches within twenty-four hours instead of two weeks or longer as demanded by most architects. (Cord controlled the manufacturing of his famous Cord automobile, the legendary Deusenberg, Checker Cab, and American Airways, progenitor of American Airlines; the home was sold to developers in 1962, torn down, and the eight-and-a-half-acre property was subdivided into thirteen lots.) As a fifty-year member of the Los Angeles Planning Commission, Williams was also influential in the design of everything from prisons to housing projects to the Hollywood YMCA, designed by his office in 1927.

His early designs were more picturesque than interesting, including both Mediterranean, Georgian, and "Olde English" themes. But by the end of the 1920s, he was beginning to experiment with a long, low, eclectic look that also defined the personality of his Spanish-derived home for Lon Chaney (1929) as well as the nearby sixteen-bedroom, twenty-two-bath Cord mansion, built soon afterward in a style owing much to Southern Colonial roots. By the mid-1930s, his business was booming, and so was the production of some of his most familiar designs, including the neo-Georgian Music Corporation of America Building, complete with two-story columns and a cupola.

He also designed homes for many stars in the 1930s and 1940s including a ten-thousand-square-foot mansion for Charles Correll (of *Amos 'n' Andy* fame), a weekend retreat at Lake Arrowhead for opera baritone John Charles Thomas; ZaSu Pitts's Brentwood home, and Barbara Stanwyck's San Fernando Valley residence. His career is also highlighted by home designs for William "Bojangles" Robinson, Eddie "Rochester" Anderson, a ranch house for Richard Arlen, and Bert Lahr's Beverly Hills home (which Williams remodeled in 1940 for bandleader Harry James). He also remodeled Jennifer Jones's home in 1946, designed Tyrone Power's Bel Air home the following year, and in 1949, was responsible for the renovation of the then celebrated Ambassador Hotel. A rustic Palm Springs getaway for Lucille Ball and Desi Arnaz followed in 1954. Twenty years earlier, he even designed a home in Hidden Hills for the man who much of the film industry loved to hate: Will Hays, Hollywood's film censor (that year he also designed the Beverly Hills home of CBS founder and chairman William Paley).

In June 1940, *Architect and Engineer* magazine, in a feature titled "Movie Stars Like Him," wrote: "Probably no one architect on the Pacific Coast has achieved greater success in domestic architecture than Mr. Williams. His work has received national recognition, a tribute particularly noteworthy in view of the handicaps which (he) faced at the beginning of his career." In 1951, Williams, who with his family had been living in a small, craftsman-style bungalow, built a house for himself and his family near today's MacArthur Park; despite its modified Regency-style entrance, he described it as "California modern" because of its horizontal bands of windows and projecting balconies. Like most of his work, which continued until his retirement in 1973, the interior was much more formal than the exterior (which also suited stars' tastes).

From 1947 to 1951, Williams designed a major remodeling of the famous Beverly Hills Hotel (intact until its recent remodeling), later followed by what many thought of at the time as the "ultimate bachelor pad" in Los Angeles' Trousdale Estates community for a between-marriages Frank Sinatra. He even designed memorials; commissioned by a local mortuary as a marketing ploy to build business, Williams produced a shrine at Hillside Memorial Park for his friend Al Jolson in 1950. For anyone who doubts how far Paul Williams traveled in a career he was first told to avoid, the irony of a black man designing a shrine for a white entertainer who first gained notoriety by performing in blackface says much.

Paul Williams died in 1980.

San Diego's Hotel del Coronado has long been a celebrity destination. The woman to the left of Charlie Chaplin is Wallis Warfield Spencer, who at the time was married to the commandant of the nearby Naval Air Station. Fifteen years later, King Edward VIII would renounce his throne to marry her. Many believe the couple first met a year before this happy afternoon when, as the Prince of Wales, the future king visited San Diego. Joining the future Duchess of Windsor are her friends Mariana Sands (*l.*) and Rhoda Fullam.

Getting Away from It All

From the very beginning, filmmaking was a tedious process, requiring actors to put in twelve-hour—or longer—days filled with seemingly endless rehearsals, takes, retakes, and set changes. So it's no wonder that, also since the beginnings of filmmaking, whenever the opportunity arose, the first thing they wanted to do is get away from it all. Then, as now, how you got away from Hollywood defined your status in the film capital as accurately as the car you drove or the splendor of the house you lived in.

And, of course, when people flew far less impulsively than is possible today, where you went was also pretty much restricted to how long it took you to get there. Despite Fatty Arbuckle's ill-fated road trip to San Francisco in 1922, during which a young "actress" named Virginia Rappe died and, because of the ensuing scandal, his career died as well, the city by the bay, four hundred miles north of Hollywood, was just too far for a short escape. Ideal, however, were three towns each a little more than one hundred miles from Los Angeles: Santa Barbara to the north, Palm Springs to the east, and San Diego to the south. In addition to offering easy escape, they also offered the option of choosing between ocean surf and desert sand.

By the late 1920s, not only were many movie stars regularly weekending away from Hollywood, some of them were even buying or building their own resorts.

Santa Barbara is today considered one of the most beautiful cities in the world. Originally popular because of its year-round moderate climate (partly a gift from nature, as its beaches, unlike those making up most of the California coastline, face directly south), it was also a major film capital during Hollywood's infancy. Although most of the once sprawling American Film Company's buildings are long gone (it was nicknamed the Flying A studio for its winged logo), still standing at the corner of Mission and Chapala Streets is an unpretentious, cream-colored building that was the studio's "green room," where actors awaited their cues to go before the cameras while filming such famous silent-era landmarks as the *Perils of Pauline* serials in the early and mid-teens. Before Santa Barbara's fledgling film industry literally "went south," Mary Pickford and Mary Miles Minter (of the William Desmond Taylor murder fame) also starred in several Flying A features, and Victor Fleming, who would one day direct *Gone with the Wind* and *The Wizard of Oz*, got his start at the studio. For what it's worth, 1916's *Purity*, the first American film containing a nude scene, was among the twelve hundred features (mostly Westerns) claimed to have been filmed there.

In 1927, construction began on what would become one of the most famous hostelries in California in a Santa Barbara suburb:

the Montecito Inn. Financed by a group of investors said to include Charles Chaplin and Arbuckle, the Mediterranean-style, three-story building adjacent to today's Pacific Coast Highway (then the Old Coast Village Road) cost three hundred thousand dollars—a huge expenditure in its day for a sixty-room inn. Its opening in February of the following year resembled a Hollywood premiere, with guests including Norma Shearer, Janet Gaynor, Wallace Beery, Carole Lombard, Gilbert Roland, and Marion Davies. In the 1950s, a pool was added, and the original wishing well that inspired Richard Rodgers and Lorenz Hart's famous 1936 love song, "There's a Small Hotel," was destroyed (it was replaced by a floral fountain in the hotel's new café that occupies the original site of the wishing well).

During the same years, Santa Barbara's El Encanto Hotel also became famous, and it still is—then for regular patrons including Hedy Lamarr, who lived there several years.

But it was to the oldest resort in Santa Barbara—in its origins one of the oldest resorts in the world—that many stars fled when they wanted anonymity: the San Ysidro Ranch. History tells us that it was founded in 1769 as a way station for the Franciscan monks traveling the Royal Road linking the California missions, and later was a five-hundred-acre citrus ranch, headquartered in an adobe house built in 1825 and now used as a private dining room. The original sandstone citrus packing plant now houses the resort's restaurant and Plow and Angel bistro.

In 1893, San Ysidro (the name, St. Isidore, honors the shepherd patron saint of Madrid) became a guest ranch, bought four decades later by actor Ronald Colman and hotelier Alvin Weingand to provide a hideaway for stars. In his time, Ronald Colman, today largely remembered for his performance as the sensitive, intellectual diplomat Robert Conway in Frank Capra's 1937 utopian film *Lost Horizon*, was born near Surrey, England, in 1891. After service in World War I, he made his professional acting debut in England and then, out of work because of the postwar Depression, moved to New York. There, his swarthy good looks got him cast in his first film opposite Lillian Gish in 1922's *The White Sister*, eventually followed by 1929's *The Dark Angel* and, famously, the escapist *Beau Geste*. After making *Arrowsmith* (based on Sinclair Lewis's novel) in 1931, Colman teamed up with his close friend Weingand for a pair of extended, round-the-world vacations during which the pair hoped to find a dream hotel to buy in the country "with a nice climate [in] a civilized area which was beautiful." The place they bought for fifty thousand in 1935 was the first stop on their second trip: Santa Barbara's San Ysidro Ranch.

Because of its solitude, assiduously guarded by the owners, the place quickly became one of Hollywood's favorite homes away from home, and stars became intensely proprietary about the place. Gloria Swanson, Merle Oberon, and David Niven demanded the same cottage whenever they visited (the Geranium Cottage); William Powell and Jean Harlow escaped the pressure-cooker environment of Hollywood in the Ranch's Magnolia Cottage; Laurence Olivier and Vivian Leigh were married there on August 30, 1940, in the ranch's wedding garden; and during a three-month stay in 1950, John Huston wrote the script for his classic film *The African Queen* there. Sinclair Lewis was once discovered by Weingand working on the revision of his novel *Ethel Bethel* in a closet: "I'd be so entranced with the view, I could not think of my characters [so] I have to work in a closet," the author explained. And perhaps most famously, John and Jacqueline Kennedy spent a week of their 1953 honeymoon in the Hillside Cottage.

Palm Springs has always been a popular destination for Hollywood celebrities, so much so that such superstars as Lucille Ball and Desi Arnaz, Bob Hope, and Frank Sinatra chose to build second homes in the resort. But for those who preferred a less permanent arrangement, the desert oasis of choice for many of the past sixty years has been the small (twenty-nine-room) Ingleside Inn. It was originally the Spanish-style estate of Humphrey Birge, owner of the Pierce Arrow Motor Car Company, which, until World War II, built what was generally considered the Rolls-Royce of American cars. The place was bought by a local councilwoman in the 1930s who transformed it into a private resort that opened only during the winter months and quickly attracted the regular patronage of dozens of stars and industry leaders, including Greta Garbo, Sam and Frances Goldwyn, Howard Hughes, Greer Garson, and opera soprano Lily Pons, who, with her husband, conductor Andre Kostelanetz, arrived for a weekend in 1952 and made it their winter home for thirteen years. That crowd was certainly tonier than that attracted to the resort and spa known as Two Bunch Palms, twenty miles north of Palm Springs. Although just about every hotel or resort that existed in Southern California during film's golden age advertises lists of celebrity guests as if they were battlefield decorations (in a sense they were and still are), few boast as their most celebrated guest not movie stars but the crime boss Al Capone, who, legend says, stayed there in the late 1920s.

1888 was a portentous year for Southern California. The great blizzard that struck New York City on March 12 of that year was one of the worst of that century or any other, and it couldn't fail but cause people to wish they lived in a more temperate climate. And, less than a month earlier, a highly attractive choice was available to them when, on February 19, the Hotel del Coronado on Coronado Island in San Diego's harbor, then the largest wooden structure outside of New York City, opened.

It didn't take long for people to put two and two together, and from the start, the five-story, Victorian "Del" (as everyone calls it today), with its then four hundred rooms, grand ballroom, and a gigantic, thirty-three-foot-high, 162-foot-long dining room, was a hit. But its fame was nothing like it would become thirty-two years later when two events took place that would make the Del one of the most popular escapes in America.

On October 28, 1919, Congress passed the Volstead Act, providing for enforcement of the Eighteenth Amendment to the Constitution, ratified nine months earlier, prohibiting the "manufacture, sale, or transportation of intoxicating liquors" in the United States. Since the hotel was less than a dozen miles from the border with Mexico, where liquor was abundant, the appeal was clear.

And, on April 7, 1920, the British battleship HMS *Renown* sailed into San Diego bearing His Royal Highness Edward Albert Christian George Andrew Patrick David Windsor, the charismatic, twenty-five-year-old Prince of Wales and heir presumptive to the Imperial British throne (the stop was not part of a state visit by the prince, as has been often reported; he was on his way to Australia, and San Diego was chosen as a recoaling port for the warship). The highlight of the one-day visit was a dinner for a thousand guests in the Del Coronado's Crown Room, hosted by the city's mayor, Louis J. Wilde.

Although it can't be proven that the prince met the wife of Lieutenant Earl Spencer, first commander of the recently established Naval Air Station on North Island adjacent to Coronado, during the visit, since it was basically the navy's show, she could've hardly failed to have been present at some of the many events that took place. In addition to the dinner at the Del, they included a public appearance in the city's Balboa Park and a reception for four hundred on board the *Renown* before the prince departed the following day. Her name, of course, was Wallis Warfield Spencer; sixteen years and another failed marriage later, she was *Time*'s infamous 1936 Person of the Year and the woman for whom the prince, then King Edward VIII, would renounce his throne on December 11 of the same year in order to marry. The couple was ever afterward known as the Duke and Duchess of Windsor. More than all the celebrities who have visited, more than all the films that have been made there, more important than the visits of ten presidents from Benjamin Harrison (who stopped by for breakfast in 1891) to Bill Clinton, the imprimatur of the royal visit made it official: The Del Coronado was the place to stay.

But of course, celebrities from Thomas Edison (who, despite rumors to the contrary, did not design the hotel's original electrical system during a visit in 1915 with his friends Henry Ford and Harvey Firestone) to Muhammad Ali already knew that; so did authors including Henry James and Ray Bradbury, and film stars from Charlie Chaplin to Madonna.

Although you'd never guess it from the hotel's marketed image, the prince never slept in the hotel—he stayed on the *Renown* while in San Diego—and was actually on its premises for perhaps three hours. Nevertheless, even today, more than eighty years after the royal visit and three generations after his abdication, the late Duke of Windsor's presence haunts the place, commemorated by the Prince of Wales restaurant and the Windsor meeting room complex to one of the actual houses in which Wallis and Earl Spencer lived while in Coronado. Moved to the hotel some twenty years ago, it now serves as a party and meeting site, opportunistically if highly inaccurately called the Windsor Cottage and situated, of course, on Windsor Green.

It even seems likely that the first movies filmed in California were a pair of short films made at the hotel in 1901 by the Edison

Moving Picture Company called *Tent City* and *The Knights of Pithias Camp*, both apparently promotional documentaries. Nothing remains of them but memories of the hotel's once popular Tent City, built on the strand south of the hotel in 1900 by John Spreckels, then the owner, to cash in on both the health craze of the era and the desire of middle-class inland Californians to escape the summer heat by taking inexpensive oceanside vacations. It was torn down in 1933.

In 1915, *Pearl of the Pacific* was made at the Del by a local production company; it was the first of more than seventy films made there, including 1929's *The Flying Fleet* starring Ramon Novarro and Anita Page; *Dive Bomber* with Errol Flynn, Fred MacMurray, and Alexis Smith a decade later; and, perhaps most famously, Billy Wilder's 1958 classic *Some Like It Hot*, which starred Marilyn Monroe, Jack Lemmon, and Tony Curtis.

Stars were staying at the Del even before they were stars. In 1950, Lucille Ball and Desi Arnaz fled Hollywood for the Del to develop and polish their Ricky and Lucy personas (with the help, it is said, of Buster Keaton), which, first tried out on the road, would a year later endear them to television audiences. While staying there, they might have caught the piano player in the hotel's Circus Room who, because audiences were so small one night, was told he could cancel his show. It was a lucky thing he didn't . . . as small as the audience was, in it was a television producer named Don Federson who realized that the pianist's ability to connect with a small audience might be perfect for the intimacy of the small screen. His stage name was Liberace.

The first celebrity visitor to the Del was Lillie Langtry in 1888, and her comments on that visit so long ago pretty well defines the hostelry's appeal since. "Its immensity astonishes me," she said, "and its perfect beauty delights me. It is so fresh and nice [and] gives such a feeling of pleasing repose." But there is a bit more to it than that, proving again that Hollywood's used and frequent abuse of coincidence is often less astonishing than real life.

Born Emilie Charlotte Le Breton on October 13, 1853, on the island of Jersey (hence her later nickname, the Jersey Lily), she married the rich Edward Langtry when she was twenty and set out to conquer society. Her stunning looks made it fairly easy for her to become the most prominent of a number of English "professional beauties," a sort of early pinup girl who sat for such painters as Whistler and Millais and lent her name and image to all kinds of products (Langtry actually owned some of the beauty products, such as hairbrushes and face powders, that used her name and image). Some of them, like Langtry, also became stage actresses.

Just before her visit to the Hotel del Coronado, Langtry, who had long since dumped her husband, bought the 4,200-acre Guenoc winery adjacent to California's Napa/Sonoma wine country and imported a winemaker from Bordeaux to grow and bottle the best claret in America; its bottles, like her beauty care products, carried a picture of her on their labels. Eventually, remarriage and a move to Monaco in 1906 ended her California adventure but not her connection with the Del Coronado, albeit indirect.

During her lifetime, Lilly Langtry attracted a diversity of male admirers including Theodore Roosevelt, Oscar Wilde, British Prime Ministers Disraeli and Gladstone, and America's own Judge Roy Bean, who named Langtry, Texas, after her. But none of them were so attracted as King Edward VII, whose mistress she became (that attraction certainly didn't extend to the besotted Edward VII's wife, Queen Alexandra, who usually referred to Langtry as "the harlot").

The coincidence? King Edward's grandson—the oldest son of Edward's son King George V and Queen Mary—was, of course, the

Hotel del Coronado's all-time prized visitor, the Prince of Wales. As long as she lived, Queen Mary, as unforgiving as her mother-in-law, Queen Alexandra when it came to male dalliance, would never forgive Wallis Warfield Spencer Simpson, once of Coronado Island, for so beguiling her son that he would give up the ancient British throne for her. Wallis may have been, as Edward VIII famously described her in his abdication radio speech, "the woman I love," but to his mother she would always be "the lowest of the low." Poor Wallis, poor Duke of Windsor, lucky Hotel del Coronado.

Index